MISFIT

SEAN MORTIMER

MISFIT

?

A Survival Guide

BALLANTINE BOOKS | NEW YORK

Ballantine Books
An imprint of Random House
A division of Penguin Random House LLC
1745 Broadway, New York, NY 10019
randomhousebooks.com
penguinrandomhouse.com

Hardcover ISBN 978-0-593-72667-9
Ebook ISBN 978-0-593-72668-6

Printed in the United States of America

1st Printing

First Edition

BOOK TEAM: Production editor: Jennifer Rodriguez • Managing editor: Pamela Alders • Production manager: Angela McNally • Copy editor: Thomas Cherwin • Proofreaders: Deborah Bader, Briony Everroad, Amy Harned

Interior art from Adobe Stock: DMM Photography Art (torn masking tape), ARTEK (abstract art), Iswanto (charcoal scribbles), miloje (textured stroke), wild (crumpled paper)

Book design by Diane Hobbing

The authorized representative in the EU for product safety and compliance is Penguin Random House Ireland, Morrison Chambers, 32 Nassau Street, Dublin D02 YH68, Ireland. https://eu-contact.penguin.ie.

FOR TONY, STACY, STECYK, KEVIN
—THANKS FOR THE DERAILMENT—

"YOU'RE WEIRD."

"SORRY."

"NO, THAT WAS A COMPLIMENT."

—DONNIE DARKO

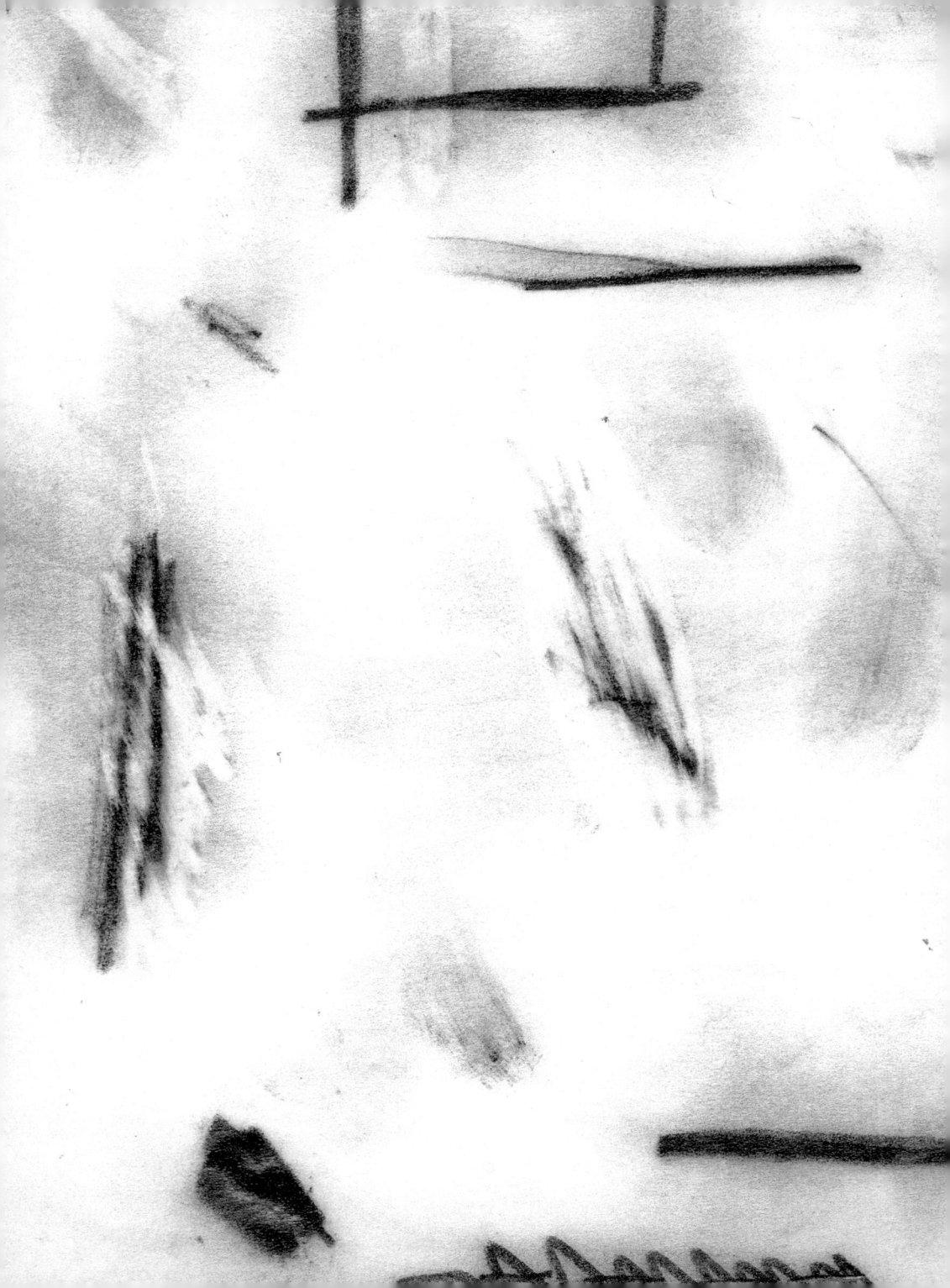

CONTENTS

Four: State of Becoming

Five: United by Dysfunction

Six: Pirate University

Seven: Hysterical Strength

Eight: Blowback

Nine: Out of the Shadows

Ten: The Dizziness of the Kook Zone

Eleven: Get a Job, Ya Bum

Twelve: The Golden Age of the Misfit

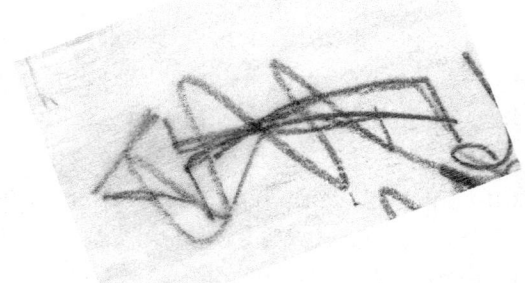

BY TONY HAWK

Skateboarding, at its core, will teach you one thing: to accept failure. Maybe even embrace it in order to learn, grow, and eventually succeed. The success can be fleeting though: Once you get a taste of progress or improvement, you'll only want more. It is this attitude that can take you further in life than you ever imagined. The amount of discipline, focus, and perseverance it takes to learn a new skate trick can seem endless. Harnessing that determination and applying it to other aspects of your life is the essence of misfit attitudes.

Sean and I grew up skating at a time when it wasn't remotely "cool" or even encouraged. But it provided us something that other sports or activities couldn't: a unique sense of self-confidence, a way to find hidden strengths, new ways to solve problems, and a sense of community within an individual pursuit. Most of the skaters I befriended in those early days are still my closest confidants, and they have all found a way to make their passions a career and a way of life.

Many subcultures have similar narratives. The pioneers of punk music did it because the mainstream crowd hated it. When snowboarding was first created, mountains banned snowboards from ski lifts because they were stigmatized by association with outcasts and misfits. Of course, all of these examples went on to reach critical mass and infiltrate mainstream media and culture in ways we could have never imagined. And the people that stuck with them found unexpected—and sometimes unwanted—success. Many of the misfits that found their passion carried that ethos into their adult responsibilities. I have met many successful entrepreneurs, artists, musicians, marketers, and chefs that credit their misfit youth with their ascension in other interests.

So take note of these life lessons, and don't be afraid to go against the grain in pursuit of something new. Turn and face the strange; it can only benefit you in the long run.

TONY HAWK—The most famous alternative sports athlete in history. Twelve-time World Skateboarding Champion. His video game franchise, *Tony Hawk's Pro Skater*, boasts sales of over a billion dollars, and his landing the 900, the first time it was ever done on live TV, was the extreme world's moon landing. This self-described misfit changed how the world thinks of sports. He attended schools where the principal confiscated his skateboard and his teacher predicted—to a guffawing class—that he would never be successful because he didn't follow the rules.

MICHElle Steilen
"estrogen"

MICHELLE STEILEN—Nicknamed "The Queen" in honor of her singular talent and role in creating modern aggro roller-skating. Michelle DIY'd the most inclusive subculture in alternative sports by starting Moxi, her street roller-skating brand. She crafted roller-skating infrastructure by founding a magazine and footwear company, and by organizing international contests for male, female, and beyond the binary. She tried really hard to be normal, it just didn't stick. "I always want to fit in!" she says. "I just can't figure it out."

SACHA
JENKINS

SACHA JENKINS—Pioneering hip-hop magazine publisher, writer, curator, musician, and documentarian (*Wu-Tang Clan, Louis Armstrong, Eminem, Hip Hop 50*, etc.). As a teenager created one of the first zines dedicated to graffiti as an art form. Early enthusiast of hardcore New York punk. Along with school-mate and soon-to-be-famous rapper Nas, received "guidance" from a high school guidance counselor that they should look at repairing refrigerators for a career.

SHEPARD FAIREY

SHEPARD FAIREY—World-famous street artist who racked up double-digit arrests as well as a space for his iconic Obama "HOPE" presidential poster in the Smithsonian's National Portrait Gallery. His international OBEY brand evolved from DIY stickers and protest prints agitating for free thinking that were "illegally" posted in public spaces into an international clothing brand. Eager to access the college screen printing room, young Shepard lied to his professor about his experience and bribed an old printer with a case of beer to DIY a rapid education in one night.

MARK
MOTHERSBAUGH

MARK MOTHERSBAUGH—Cofounder of DEVO, a "weirdo" band that helped introduce "alternative" music to the world. Part of the historic Kent State protests where four students were killed by the National Guard, Mark made a soundtrack to the devolution around him. Today he is one of the most successful movie, TV, and video game composers, making unconventional music for *Thor: Ragnarok, Pee-wee's Playhouse, Regular Show, What We Do in the Shadows, Crash Bandicoot, The Sims 2,* etc. Nobody, including Mark, realized he was legally blind until he was seven.

ROGUES' GALLERY

ROGER
GASTMAN

ROGER GASTMAN—Seduced by the East Coast's underground graffiti scene, Roger became the world's foremost expert on the street art displayed on exterior walls and trains. His Beyond the Streets art exhibits celebrate "mark makers and rule breakers" by hosting multimillion-dollar exhibits in NYC, London, Shanghai, and LA. The *Los Angeles Times* noted how an early art show of Roger's drew "the ire of social critics, alarmed by what they perceive as an institutional celebration of vandalism."

SENECA—The artist specializing in trippy art is also responsible for the look of the "Bored Ape" that grew to epitomize the billion-dollar surge with NFTs (non-fungible tokens). Riffing on the existential boredom of mega-rich Silicon Valley dot-commers, her "creativity helped fuel a technological revolution," according to *Rolling Stone* magazine. Her creativity and identity are shaped by chronic lucid nightmares.

SENECA

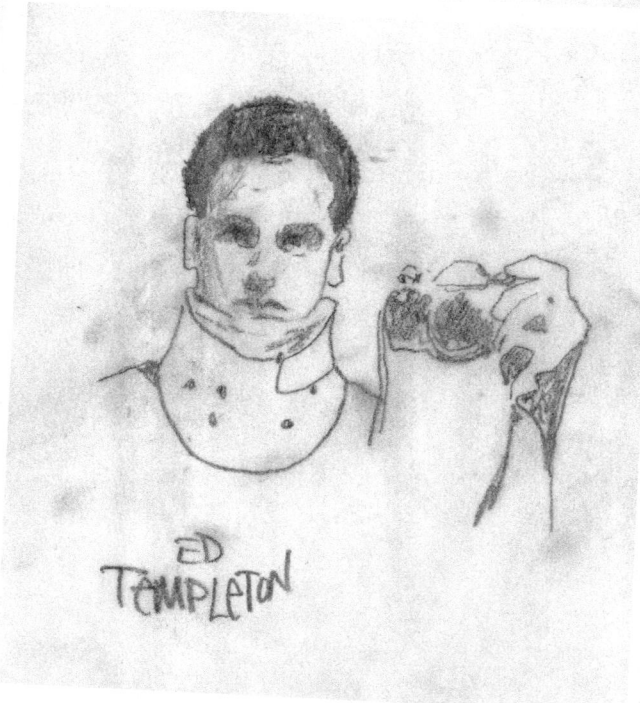

ED
TEMPLETON

ED TEMPLETON—One of the most famous street skateboarders is also an acclaimed contemporary artist and photographer, with pieces in MOMA and worldwide gallery shows. His Toy Machine skateboard brand is a leaning lighthouse for subversive messaging in these days of sterile Olympic embrace. The award-winning photographer is regularly hired to shoot high-end fashion brands, but is known to reject the six-figure checks when grossed out by the brand's vibe.

DR. JoN 1

DR. JON FREEMAN—One might assume that a successful psychotherapist running a Manhattan neuroscience research facility would be satisfied, but Dr. Jon gave it all up to start The Brooklyn Strategist. The community-based game center welcomes all kinds of misfits while developing an enrichment program based on board games that had stereotypically guaranteed a life of escapism and abuse in high school. Teenage Jon's parents insisted on bringing in professional help because they thought playing Dungeons & Dragons was swaying him into Satan's dark embrace.

STACY PERALTA—World champion skateboarder, award-winning filmmaker, and creative power behind the Bones Brigade, the most impactful team in alternative sports. Stacy had the best-selling skateboard in the world, discovered Tony Hawk, and made the first action sports video. His later mainstream documentaries focus on outsider cultures like surfing, LA gangs, and skateboarding. Stacy once hid in a tree to successfully evade arrest.

STACY PERALTA

With cameos by . . .

C.R. STECYK III—The conceptual artist with pieces in MOMA and the Smithsonian is also an acclaimed participant in various subcultures, cultural shaper, and historian. As a prank he buried a bomb prop on a busy beach and returned on the busiest day of the year in a bomb disposal uniform to dig it up. Chaos ensued.

BRIAN FLYNN—Owner of Super7, one of the largest alternative toy brands, with a focus on fringe outsider vibes, including series called The Weirdest and The Worst with posable action figures like Trauma Bomb.

MAT HOFFMAN—World champion BMXer, X Games gold medalist, *Jackass* star, and a most hardcore human who has survived over fifty surgeries and flatlined twice.

MISFIT

It is a brutal moment of realization. You immediately recognize that there will be no way to deflect the damage. Your cold acceptance of an inescapable situation flicks you into a disorientating spin, spiraling into an isolated space where all navigation equipment is rendered useless.

There is no loving parent capable of hugging the dread away. Finally, the realization sinks in: You are the problem, not them.

In a society built for people conforming, you are incapable of fitting in.

You mis-fit.

ONE

MOMMY, WHY AM I WEIRD?

Wait, Instructions Aren't Included?

I don't know about you, but life didn't go on for too long before I felt an abrupt awkwardness, like I was an irregular jigsaw piece failing to snap together cleanly with others.

Laughing at an absurd social situation that draws puzzled looks from others. Getting peeled from conversations about mainstream interests after struggling to muster attentiveness. Dropping a contextual movie line from a cult film—"Yeah, yeah! Let's go get sushi and not pay."—comes off as troubling, obscure and random, perhaps indicative of an apparent neurological tic.

How exactly did this stray jigsaw piece find its way into the wrong puzzle box again?

The world loves to celebrate misfits—*after* the fact. *Oh, look at the inexhaustible strength of the independent hero charging from the fringe!* Tales are retold, obstacles are enlarged, troops inspired, unconventional beliefs put into practice until they swirl into mythological quests. Huckleberry Finn. Luke Skywalker. Lady Gaga. Einstein. Joan of Arc. Bowie. Tony Hawk. Galileo. David Lynch. Cyndi Lauper. Johnny Rotten. Sinéad O'Connor. Cool Hand Luke. Wu-Tang Clan. Dalí. RuPaul. Frida

Kahlo. Kurt Cobain. Basquiat. Bob Dylan. Lil Nas X. Patti Smith. Billie Eilish. The focus shining on how their seemingly supernatural force of will blasted the weird, the unconventional, the alternative, the counter-culture into conventional society. In hindsight, how could they not mutate the world?

As a culture, we celebrate tales of underdog victory, concealing a defining characteristic of the misfit journey—*the fact that no misfit starts the game by choice.* All the misfits I've known—from ragamuffin artists to awkward kids at Magic: The Gathering game nights to bouncing hyper-pop avant-gardists to world-famous oddballs who changed mainstream perceptions of music, sports, and art—started off trying to fit in. *Desperately.* And we all sucked at it.

"Underdog" suggests playing a game against a favored opponent, as if we all agreed to the rules, shook hands to assure sportsmanship, and voluntarily stepped across the chalked line on the field competing for a shared idea of a win.

The harsh truth is, in the beginning, misfitting is anything but a conscious choice to play a game with clearly defined rules. Nobody inflicts this level of personality-shredding rejection on themselves if they have another option.

But veteran misfits know it's a force necessary to eject us out of conventionality. It's the first painful step on the misfit journey, though it feels more like a sucker punch followed by a shove off a cliff. You find yourself dazed, bruised, and in unfamiliar territory, forced to take an unconventional and often painful trip.

Speaking from experience, the sense of disorientation and disconnection at this point is sickening. Uncertainty, panic, and fear mix to create some seriously rancid emotions. But that changes when you realize how these outcast discomforts serve a purpose.

That said, you're still going to have to slog through the emotional and social muck. You're going to get lost and get cold and, out of an ugly desperation, be forced to discover new pathways. Obstacles will intentionally be placed on your path. The promise of control and security that makes conformity so addicting will be startlingly absent until you realize that **what had felt like a broken compass leading you astray was pointing in a very specific direction.**

If this book does anything, I hope it brings an understanding of how to use your misunderstood navigational tool. First you'll learn how to traverse this strange, unfamiliar landscape. Then you will progress to mapping your own unique path as confusion transforms into confidence.

This book explores the experiences of a diverse group of misfits to collect shared survival skills that can help outcasts of all kinds, regardless of labels like age and gender or where you are in your journey through nonconformity. The quickest way to expire in a wilderness is to panic. Knowing that others were exactly where you are and made it out rouses hope and possibility. At the very least, I hope this book offers some company when it feels the loneliest.

Spoiler alert—the misfit journey never ends. Regardless of age and circumstances, every misfit must still interact with a society nursing a hardcore addiction to conformity. **But know that it is possible to not only survive but thrive with your oddball self.**

My more experienced misfit friends and I still find ourselves in circumstances where we feel socially rejected. The difference is that now, instead of cratering our self-confidence, it produces a pleasurable sting of awareness that tugs a small smile. In those moments, not fitting in reminds us of what we've earned. What used to feel like a curse now fizzes with effervescent gratitude. We understand the joys of misfitting.

Land of confusion

When conversations with misfits touch on childhood, a familiar origin story emerges. I'm not sure if it can be attributed to mutation of the DNA code, residue of a rebellious reincarnation, or some spicy spiritual ingredients peppered in right before birth. Whatever it may be, early on there is an unsettling awareness that our social magnets were inserted incorrectly. The poles repelled rather than attracting and snapping together like everyone else's. Often, before understanding there is recognition: *What is this bewildering part of me that sparks to life and prompts me to take ridiculous stands against seemingly banal traditional asks?*

This is a heady question to tumble around a child's head, and reactions can span the spectrum. I cried a lot as a kid. Then I became a teenager and punched holes in my bedroom door. Confusing frustration leading to lashing out is a common theme with future misfits.

I helped Tony Hawk, the painfully skinny outcast kid who became the famous face of a renegade misfit activity still technically illegal in most cities—aka skateboarding—write his biography, and we called an early section "Demon Boy." His mother once told me how a babysitter grew concerned over the toddler's rage. Tony, sentenced to a stint in the crib, let his caretaker know what he thought about her authority. "She told me how Tony would scrunch his face up and throw his toy cars at her from his crib," Mrs. Hawk said. "She really cared for Tony, but eventually left because the relationship wasn't healthy for a developing child."

When Tony left behind the crib, things didn't change that much. Mrs. Hawk tried to teach him to play tennis, only to clue in to her son's idea of the game after being tagged by balls a few times. "Tony, I think you're trying to hit me." To him it seemed like a sound strategy.

Even if they weren't forced to participate in traditional athletics, future world champion misfits found ways to rebel. "I really got into a lot of mischief as a kid," Stacy Peralta, Tony's early mentor, says. The former pro skateboarder and current award-winning documentarian describes a childhood that makes it obvious why he and Tony connected. "I really loved throwing fruit at passing cars, dirt clods at windows. I was always getting into trouble. There was no mean intent—I had a very active imagination and was always having fun. I was always building things, doing models and very industrious, but I was always in trouble—I wanted to play."

Oh, like play baseball in a uniform running along chalked lines with umpires and cheering parents?

Nope.

"I wanted to stick firecrackers in apples and throw them and see them explode in the air," Stacy clarifies. "It was so much fun to have an orange explode on the roof of a passing car. To see a dirt clod break apart on a plate glass window and not break the window? That was like art.

Cops came to my house three times, not for anything bad, just that I blew a firecracker off in some lady's windowsill."

As humans, we are not wired to be stoked about being cast off and alone. Shame. Guilt. Anxiety. Fear. Anger. Regret. **Take a whack at the elaborate piñata that is the misfit brain and see what awkward emotional assortments scatter across the ground.** Even when one isn't inclined to express inner feelings with rotting fruit or toy car projectiles, those same feelings can corkscrew inward. Stomachaches, hyper-competitiveness, panic, tears, fears, anxiety, anger, isolation, crumbling self-confidence. When there are no instructions included, no premade mold to pour emotions into, they have a habit of spilling all over the place.

The artist Seneca specializes in wonderfully tripped-out images as well as being the lead designer behind the infamous "Bored Ape" NFT character. Considering her staid family background, it says something that when given free rein, she used an emotionally vapid primate to create a wicked caricature of ennui, that untranslatable French word describing a particular flavor of soul-crushing, blown-out boredom.

"I come from a really traditional Chinese family," she says, "which means certain rituals or beliefs and values stem from generations past and are very strictly enforced. I was a good daughter, or at least I really tried to be." Good-daughter attempts aside, the same frictional heat that Tony and Stacy felt burned within her and found no outlet. "I did it all, whatever my parents wanted me to do, but I definitely wasn't happy and that definitely trickled into some of my clinical anxiety and all that shit."

Tangled up with the anger and angst is a state of absurdity, an off-balance world where everyone else appears to have studied an operational manual that you never received. Michelle Steilen, aka Estro Jen, would go on to become one of the most influential female alternative athletes, but when she was six her babysitter said, 'My daughter is going to be cheerleading, do you want to go?' I had no idea what cheerleading was."

She shrugged and went along, unaware she was entering a world of misfit confusion. "I was super into using my energy and the stunts, the flipping, the jumping, but I didn't really understand what we were doing for a long time. What was the purpose of the cheerleader? Why are we doing this? Why aren't we watching what is going on? Why are we facing the crowd? We don't need to encourage these people—the game is already happening."

Michelle was temporarily affixed with a cheerleader label, but it didn't provide a soothing sense of identity. At first it seems as if misfits, by their very nature, do not instinctively know how to build an identity, but it may be more accurate to say that early outcasts have something in them arguing for a wider choice rather than automatically accepting available generic identities. The problem is that at this point in our development we're not clear why we are operating this way or what it is that we want.

"What's your problem?" is a question many starter misfits hear on the regular, sometimes asked in the true spirit of discovery but often in annoyance and exasperation. I know I'm a misfit and that this may be the problem, but, really, is there a way to answer that? Trust me, as a kid trying to fit in, if I'd had control over what I was doing wrongly, I'd have stopped doing it. Having people constantly question the motivation behind your incorrectness can put you into a perpetual self-interrogation loop: Do regular people know what is wrong with them? Is not knowing what is wrong what makes you wrong? How does everyone else even know what is considered wrong to begin with?

It was a loop I found myself in throughout my childhood. Mind you, I had some help. My first memory of life is standing in the rain at age two-point-five, holding my mom's hand and waiting for the short yellow bus to pick me up for an hour ride to the diagnostic center. I didn't know what was wrong, but apparently everyone else did. The average infant says their first word by age one and my parents were still waiting for mine to cross the finish line. That early misfit frustration manifests in the most basic way when you are old enough to know what you want yet unable to communicate it.

The rain would have been melodramatic if I didn't live in Vancouver, Canada, where it rains more than half the year, and the short bus would be a tasteless joke if it hadn't been needed to take me to therapists to help me say my first word. For the hour-long bus ride, I marinated in how so many people were trying to fix me. Too young for comparative analysis, I wasn't aware of what "normal" was, but I was aware of how my emotions fluctuated between explosions of uncontrollable anxiety at the diagnostic center or implosions into states of dissociated numbness. What do you do when what makes you you is the problem?

MARK MOTHERSBAUGH "I'll tell you what happened to me as a kid. Everyone thought I was a super-intense weirdo. I'd hear somebody at the door and run up and get really close and be six inches from their face and yell, 'Grandma!' or whoever it was. I didn't obey the social distancing that everybody else was being taught as you grow up. You know, as a human, you have to learn that stuff.

"At school the teacher would say, 'Mark, add up the numbers on the board.' I'd say, 'What's a board?' and everybody would laugh and the teacher would say, 'All right, smart kid—get in the back!' I was forced to sit in a corner. I couldn't figure it out—how do people know the right thing to say?

"At the end of second grade the teacher who had been punishing me all year saw me trying to read a book with my face smashed against the pages. She asked my parents if I'd ever had my vision tested. They said no and she said I might need glasses. I went and took the eye exam and couldn't see the first letter, the big E on an eye chart, if it was further than six inches away. The optometrist said, 'You know your son is legally blind?' My parents were like, 'What? Huh?'

"A couple of weeks later I got my first pair of glasses. Back in those days the lenses for extreme myopia looked like the bottom of a glass Coke bottle, but I saw telephone wires, clouds, birds in the sky for the first time. I'd never seen the sun before. I'd never seen the tops of trees—I only knew the parts that I ran into. I knew the path and the sidewalk to get to school—I had walked it for two years—but I never knew what my school looked like.

"I had thought everybody saw the way I did. I had no way to gauge what having vision further than six inches away was like and thought other kids knew things that I didn't know. I never thought I was atypical—everyone else just thought I was strange."

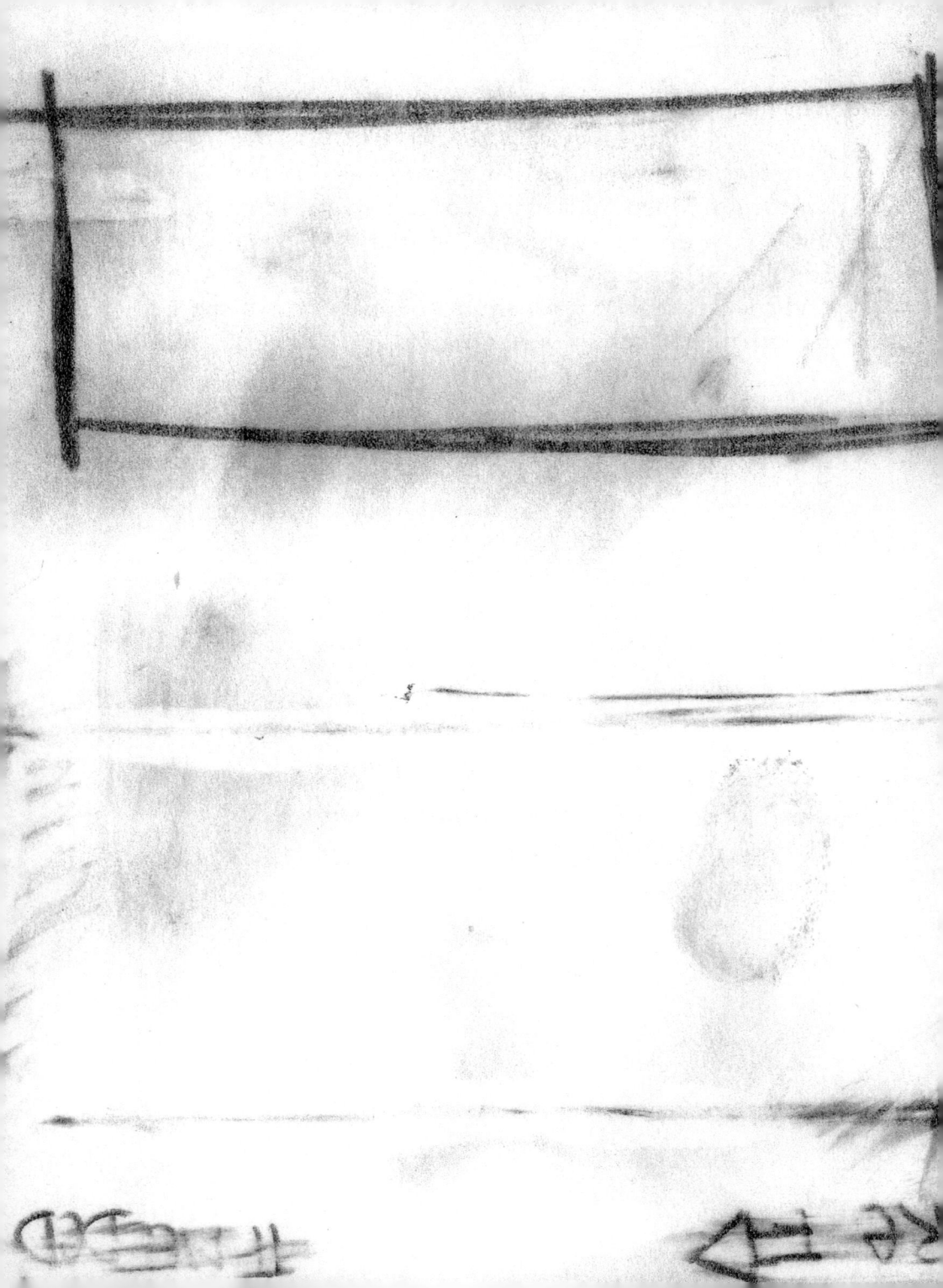

2

Under the Paving Stones, the Beach!

We've established that misfitting doesn't start with intent, but is bewilderingly passive—"I'm not sure *why* I'm not like them." But for all of us on the misfit journey, there comes a time when incapacity to conform metamorphoses into rebellion. It can hit strange, an undesired evolution that you didn't know you were working toward, but once the impulse *not* to conform appears, suddenly it becomes impossible to ignore.

Your reaction may present as quiet rebellion, an inward steeling of resolve, or outward aggression. Either way you will feel an inner force channeling itself in new ways, a shot of outcast adrenaline flashing through you to help deal with the situation. At this point it may not accomplish anything, but it is the first taste of misfit power that will help push you through the many thresholds ahead of you.

There is a famous black-and-white picture of rioting in 1968 France in which a casually dressed young man charges in front of a crowd and hurls a brick with all his might at an unseen opposing force, literally dismantling society's structure by repurposing the paving stone into a weapon of protest—his body graceful, his face relaxed and calmly focused, his whole essence zeroed in on this act of insubordination. There is French graffiti attached to this protest: *Sous les pavés, la plage!* In English: Under the paving stones, the beach!

I had no clue what motivated the brick-throwing beef when I first saw the older picture at age seven, but this dynamic image of civil disobedience personified a rebellious aspect of myself that I did not yet know. My inner brick thrower, the protesting part of me, seethed with dedication and confidence so complete that I knew they were there for protective reasons. Indeed, few things in my relatively short life had arrived with such conviction. But, like most brick-throwing incidents, it created turmoil, unintended consequences. *Throw bricks enough and things you never aimed for have a habit of ending up broken.*

As a second-grader I had finally learned how to talk, albeit a struggle with articulation made me sometimes sound like a sloshed European. I had waited all week for a classmate's birthday, Pavlovian drool already pooling over the upcoming sugar intake, with the bottomless soda, cake, potato chips, and goody bags full of even more rare treats. I grew up in a small fishing village outside of Vancouver with a mom who baked brown bread and bought the peanut butter with no sugar, and for me birthday parties ran a close second to Halloween.

Ten minutes or so before mass sugar consumption, my mom came into my room and told me to get ready. "I am ready." She shook her head, instructing me to put on an ironed navy-blue turtleneck, explaining how it was appropriate attire for a party and showed respect.

My inner French protester appeared out of nowhere, pulled up some of the paving stones, and began pitching. Defiance sparked and an emotional dumpster fire heated my belly as I shook my head. Mom wasn't backing down, and I stared holes through her as she told me to hurry up so I could get going. For her, this was nothing more than a casual ask. In

the recent past that exact turtleneck had been pulled over my head without issue, but something about this time, for a reason that remained so coded and complex that surface me could not decipher, never mind articulate, was different. I followed her out of my room, stomping down the stairs, arguing all the way into the kitchen, realizing that Turtleneck Ridge was a hill I was prepared to die on.

My mom clearly thought I was being a brat, that this was no big deal, and told me to march back up there and get that turtleneck on. I could tell that she wasn't going to back down, but I also felt the friction inside as I dug in at some disconnected spiritual level and continued arguing. Belly heat radiated, generating the emotional equivalent of sugar-rush energy to fuel furious brick pitching at the relative omnipotence of parental authority. Various argumentative techniques were employed, all ending in failure.

I knew the rules of the game. **They were forcing me to do something— "they" being teachers, parents, authority figures—explaining rules about the "proper" way to behave, to look, to act.**

I never said no to my parents when asked to do a chore. There was complaining aplenty, attempts at shirking work details, but never outright refusal. I understood and respected the chain of command. My parents were not perfect, but they were pretty awesome, disciplined but understanding, so there wasn't the option of simply refusing to wear the turtleneck and getting my way. My kid brain crunched the data and knew the answer.

I had lost.

But this wasn't simply a matter of winning or losing—it had slipped onto another emotional frequency for me, the stakes somehow much more fundamental. My inner brick thrower had taken a mild disagreement and escalated it until my nervous system regarded it as an existential battle. The more chill part of me was never invited to discuss the situation with my inner agitator, so there was zero understanding as to how I found myself in a flight-or-fight response. Who was this foreign agitator throwing bricks *at* exactly?

I quietly exited the kitchen and walked back up the stairs, ritualistically taking off my T-shirt as I entered my room and began climbing my chest of drawers. The most dominant piece of furniture in my bedroom, it was angled against a far corner, leaving a clean empty triangle of solitude behind it. I climbed slowly, careful not to provide any audible clues, shimmied down the back, and curled up at the bottom.

Time plays differently to kids, and I have no idea how long it took for my mom to get suspicious and walk into the room and then around the house calling my name, warning me that I was going to be late for the party. I didn't say anything. I had never hidden or ignored my mom before, but by now, none of this was directed at her. I was going to make myself not exist—and even more surprising to me, I didn't want to go to the party anymore. I was fine with not having any of it, energy settling into a weird flatness after an all-encompassing emotional jettison.

My inner French protester had put down the bricks and was probably leaning against a lamppost, looking cool, biting off chunks of a baguette in between drags off his Gauloises. The brick throwing had forced change, a measure of success in any protest. The turtleneck didn't even exist anymore—it had simply been a vehicle to carry the message.

It had always felt as if early childhood was a wondrous open range of spontaneous landscapes where you were free to wander, climb, and log-roll down into various levels of discovery. And then conventional culture corralled you into its manicured field of play complete with pre-drawn, pre-measured, preordained chalk lines, spectating crowds cheering or

booing, refs blowing whistles announcing infractions, giant scoreboard up high for everybody to monitor.

You don't even need the power of metaphor to emphasize the misfit reaction to mandated regulation. "I never understood team sports," Stacy said in the raw interview for the Bones Brigade documentary, a film about the most celebrated skateboard team in history. "I didn't understand the whistles and the referees and these grids and lines. 'You can't go here and you're offside there and you're out of bounds here.' I just didn't get that stuff, and it was intimidating to me."

Winner or loser? Right or wrong? Polite or rude? Normal or irregular? Accepted or rejected? Binary placement suddenly seems a main objective behind a lot of new situations forced upon us. Being drafted without consent into a conformist game and then having the results provide a metric of worth and identity felt inescapable. **People in charge kept acting as if I had freedom of choice: winner or loser, you pick.**

But the turtleneck had burst this constrained sense of choice, illuminating a solution so out in the open that it was baffling how I had missed it. *Win or lose? Couldn't you simply not play?* Turn and walk off the field, "light out for the Territory ahead of the rest," as Huck Finn put it before he bounced at the end of his book?

It was scary and isolating to take myself out of the game, but choosing marginalization rather than having it imposed made a transcendent difference. I didn't feel like a quitter, because I'd never agreed to play the game to begin with. I didn't know where I was going, except off the field, alone.

Curled up shirtless in my triangle of solitude, I was transported into another emotional state. At least anger had provided a sense of companionship. I hadn't asked for this, yet here I was in an emptiness that while foreboding was also mysterious, like an empty container awaiting something unknown to fill it.

My mom eventually looked behind the chest of drawers, and I can still remember how long the distance appeared as I looked up and said I wasn't going to the party. I was calm, at peace. The cake and candy and soda seemed suddenly priced differently, and the cost seemed too much. All I knew was that I couldn't afford it.

TONY HAWK "I did team sports mostly because it was expected, tradition. At some point, I realized that I didn't really enjoy it like my friends enjoyed it. I didn't like relying on the team. I didn't like the team relying on me. I didn't want to have to depend on the team and I didn't want to let anyone down. The first time I ever played baseball, I imagined hitting a home run or at the very least a double. I went up to bat and struck out. It was not what I imagined or was prepared for. Failure wasn't on my radar, so to have failed in an instant? I was like . . . what just happened? No one told me this could happen, and even if they did, I probably wasn't going to listen. Immediately, I ran off the field into a canyon and hid.

"My dad coaxed me out and the rest of the team was, 'What the fuck? It's not even a big deal.' But it felt like a big deal. And, it was the 1970s so bullying was rampant. Was there a support system after I reacted so emotionally? Yeah, right . . . Are you asking if they were empathetic? The answer is no."

TWO

ENTER THE
THUNDERDOME

3

What's This "Normal" Thing You Keep Talking About?

STACY PERALTA "School didn't interest me—it couldn't compete with my imagination. Other than art, I found it so tedious and boring. At the time, I computed that as 'I'm dumb.' I couldn't lock my attention on it—it was just so boring and I felt no connection to it.

"I'd spend all my time at school waiting for that clock to count down because I couldn't wait to get home and dive into my things. I was very good at learning things and focusing on things, but only if they interested me. But the interests that drew me to them? I was never given any positive feedback in pursuing them."

isfit," as any misfit knows, is a relative label. There are no universal characteristics that define the term. It's a designation that requires a large amount of other people pieces snapping into place and when enough fit together they manifest their own unit. And guess what, oddball? You ain't fitting into that. Weirdo.

Not fitting in is dependent on others, usually a majority in both percentage and power. As Weezer sang in the song "In the Garage," there is no misfitting when alone in your own space: "In the garage, I feel safe / No one cares about my ways / In the garage where I belong / No one hears me sing this song." As outcasts we are defined by what we are not, which is "normal," so let's examine that term in a misfit manner.

What is normal when you think about it? It's bandied about as a known quality, some universal baseline, an elemental truth, but that is a fiction. So how is the concept even formed? Writing and deleting lines for forty minutes on this page made me realize that I have no idea how to even conceptualize the idea of normal, so I gave up and searched Dictionary.com.

NORMAL: *Conforming to the standard or the common type; usual; not abnormal; regular; natural.*

Whoa.

Harsh.

First word drops the hammer: "*Conforming.*" No wonder you're not inclined to be normal.

In 1964 the Supreme Court heard a case about a movie theater showing a foreign flick that some saw as French art and some saw as a hardcore porno with annoying subtitles that got in the way. In deciding the case, Justice Potter Stewart deployed the infamous "I know it when I see it" ruling.

"I shall not today attempt further to define the kinds of material I understand to be embraced within that shorthand description [pornog-

raphy], and perhaps I could never succeed in intelligibly doing so. But *I know it when I see it.*"

Normal sounds more like pornography now that I think about it. Substitute "normal" for "porno" and you get a sense of how arbitrarily the general public defines abnormal behavior: "when they see it." The problem being that people peeping the exact same thing often see very different realities, and a common refrain of beginner misfits is not seeing things the way the majority does.

"I thought everybody saw the way I did," legally blind Mark said earlier, echoing a timeless sentiment of starter misfits, even ones with twenty-twenty vision.

Besides being blind as a bat, Mark grew up in one of the most socially conformist eras in modern history. Planted in the postwar American heartland of Ohio, where middle-class domestication was a newfangled national fad, Mark would go on to cofound DEVO, a band that helped usher in "alternative" music.

When the celebrated band played live on *SNL,* stage to some of the biggest rock star swagger on television, they wore yellow hazmat suits, oversized disposable safety glasses, and moved like malfunctioning Disney robots. If there was rock and roll school, DEVO would be owning the freaks and geeks table in the far corner of the cafeteria.

The band's message is so powerful that Kurt Cobain, a misfit leader himself in the 1990s as lead singer of Nirvana, not only covered a DEVO song, but also stated: "Of all the bands who came from the underground and made it in the mainstream, DEVO were the most challenging and subversive of all." With misfit cred like that, you can probably guess where Mark's childhood falls on the normal scale.

Pre-glasses, Mark remembers being on a playground and incoming baseballs appearing more like supersonic rockets. Traditional athletic projectiles zoomed out of an impenetrable visual fog, sharpening into focus only at the very last moment like V2 rockets, velocity undetermined because Mark had no sense of range.

Little Mark's mind didn't think he had irregular eyes, it assumed *everybody else* had figured out how to catch a V2 baseball. "I had no way to gauge what having vision that saw further than six inches away was like," he says. Likewise, everybody else that was "normal" thought Little Mark saw like them—that, in other words, he *really* sucked at baseball.

At a distance, it seems natural for the social order to create a communal baseline, manifesting a group definition of "normal." Most kids saw well enough to catch a baseball, so nobody involved thought to explore what, or how, Mark saw. **The assumption being that my "normal" is your "normal," but not understanding that "normal" is the common loose thread running through all our young misfit sweaters, one that conformists usually find incapable of pulling.**

Even though I had learned to talk by second grade, it was clear that my brain was a different model than the standard version when I looked at words. Every day in elementary school my class had to go to a communal table and pick a chapter book for silent reading. As the only one in my class barely reading at a kindergarten level, I was well aware that I wasn't normal. I also recognized that the entire class knew who the single thick cardboard-paged "baby book" at the table was for—the kid that said "foo" when trying to say "flu."

When you are behind in school or social norms, you are well aware of what is a learned skill, like reading, because it seems *impossible* to learn. But I was an escape artist and, unable to sequence sounds into words, I began memorizing entire pages with the volunteer parents who took me out into the hallway for reading help. Eventually, I was caught when my finger underlining the words didn't match up.

Now, were they impressed that my brain could memorize entire pages and spit them back? Did they notice that and maybe think I might learn to read by sight rather than phonetically, the "normal" way? Spoiler: No. And through every remedial book and tearful spelling test for the next few years, they taught me that not only was I dumb, but I was also failing to learn how to be normal.

For the first chunk of childhood, most of us are wonderfully unaware of what "normal" children are up to outside the home perimeter, but as the frequency of structured social activities like school and organized sports increases, so does a growing suspicion that something is rotten in the state of Denmark.

As rule-bound communal activities increase, an odor can begin permeating the new common areas, and it seems as if only you and other misfits can smell it. Normal becomes mandated to a certain degree, and weirdo tendencies begin to blip alarmingly on authority's radar screen. Labels such as "peculiar," "abnormal," "curious," "odd," "atypical," "eccentric," "strange," and "weird" are now pinned to non-normies with real-world consequences, the start of formative identities. "All my teachers would say I was a distraction in class," Michelle remembers.

"It was pretty common to do something and get a harsh reaction in school," Mark says. "The teacher would ask a question and I'd answer with something that would make people laugh. When the teacher would discipline me, **I'd be thinking,** *How do the other kids know the* **right** *thing to say?* The whole world could feel like that. But you can just stumble through life and people will push you through to the next thing and the next place." It's as if misfits have a blind spot that hides how the surrounding majority make snap decisions and judgments about what is normal.

The artist, historian, surfer, and OG skateboarder C.R. Stecyk III would go on to have pieces displayed by the Smithsonian, MOMA, and even the White House. As a child he was taught by "women in bat costumes," aka Catholic nuns. When they instructed the class to paint a barn, he went at it like always, totally oblivious to conformist, boxed thinking. When it came time to survey the collective pieces of art, one was unlike all the others. A classroom full of red barns and blue skies had an interloper with a distinct purple barn and ominous black sky. "Alarm bells went off," Stecyk said in an interview. "There were tests and stuff." By "tests," Stecyk is referring to psychological evaluations.

The problem often compounds into an absurd state where you are so far off the traditional path—so "behind," as guardians of the status quo like to say—that you completely lose track of the route that everyone else is taking to Normalville. My childhood and early teenage years were stacked with experiences of trying to comprehend what everybody else grasped effortlessly, but I'd sit there like a dog tilting its head trying to understand.

Mark's inability to see much of anything farther than six inches away for his first seven years and thinking that was normal "put me off on a weird start to life," he says. "It sent me in a different trajectory." But there doesn't have to be an identifiable "error" that causes a misfire. Misfits go sideways regardless of how typical our life started off. A misfit's brain appears calibrated differently, with an overactive fence-climbing curiosity, perspective dialed into divergent horizon lines, and processing that produces questions instead of blank obedience.

We can be mad inquisitive in a way that "puts a battery in your back," as graffiti and hip-hop publisher and documentarian Sacha Jenkins puts it. **The outcasts I know treat life as a riddle demanding inventive, perspective-altering solutions rather than a standardized test with rote answers.** But, sooner or later, most misfits get shoved into a system where rote answers and rigid definitions are not only required but play a part in social identity. When a child is put into an activity with twenty

other kids and a single grading system, it teaches us in real time how concepts of normal and abnormal manifest.

Mark got glasses and saw a whole new world—could that correction finally make him normal? "Then a girl asked why my head was shaped like a light bulb," he says. "I looked in the mirror and my head *was* shaped like a light bulb! I had a big head and a tiny body and thick glasses. From then on, I was acutely aware that I didn't look like other people."

Fantastic. Now that Mark could see like everyone else, he was finally able to see that his head was all wrong. "I didn't feel that I fit in," Mark and every other misfit says, finally learning the lesson being taught.

Let's be clear about one thing—misfits are not calmly sitting at the sorting table taking in each instruction and interaction, unemotionally reviewing reactions, and objectively picking the unpopular one purposefully, thus "bringing it on themselves," as so many defenders of convention like to frame it. **That line of thinking and lack of empathy is like throwing a person who can't swim into the middle of the ocean and telling them they're making a choice by drowning instead of swimming.**

Being baffled by what the majority considers normal isn't necessarily limited to inflexible scholastic styles—the general construct of traditional activities can reveal an almost dyslexic issue with widespread conventionality. "I played Little League one year when I was about nine years old," Stacy said in an interview. "I remember going up to bat for the first time and seeing how fast that ball passed the plate. I actually backed up three feet. I was terrified. I was an ice sculpture at the plate. I was too scared to swing. That went over very well with my teammates."

Another iconic alternative athlete, Michelle Steilen, looked at the organized games around her childhood and, unlike Justice Potter Stewart, did not know what she was seeing. Michelle would go on to make a roller-skating video viewed millions of times, but as a kid understanding why other girls her age were wearing uniforms and kicking a ball around while somebody whistled rules? Nada. "I didn't play traditional sports as a kid," she says, remembering falling into the misfit tendency of asking a million questions about why somebody would do something while normal kids were fine with being told to run around numbered things called "bases." She laughs, forehead crinkling in puzzlement remembering the confusion. "I didn't understand them."

It can be cool for somebody like Michelle who is now celebrated for her unconventionality to front being so above all the normal junk, but there was real confusion and pain at the time. Michelle is an awesome beacon of oddball inclusivity, detectable at a far distance. How she roller skates everywhere, smiles, greets people, dresses, waves her arms around, gets embarrassed, and talks to herself all make it clear why she has such an impressive and passionate worldwide following. What makes Michelle so inviting is a vulnerability that has become a source of power. She's not shooting for hipster cool. "I always want to fit in!" she says, as if it were the most obvious thing in life. "I just can't figure it out."

Even when misfits are successful in early organized traditional group activities, they can find ways to make the fit awkward. By age seven I ran faster and longer than anyone else at my school, winning the elementary school running award with over 180 miles. I assume I was okay at soccer, because I played it and I have seen photos my mom took, but my brain only bothered holding on to one memory of any time on the field, which was when I rode my bike across it to quit.

When I refused to play soccer anymore, my mom made me tell the coach and the team in person as a sign of respect. I didn't understand all the emotions stirred up around soccer games and I hated the team aspect of it, becoming stressed to the point of tears over letting people down,

MISFIT

but I understood the respect part. I was fine with quitting in person . . . as long as I first applied KISS makeup, specifically Ace Frehley's "Starman" design: black outlined silver stars around each eye, face whited out, black lipstick.

I was totally confused as to why the heck I would need to do this, but something inside of me, that inner brick thrower, demanded it as an active ingredient in the recipe of the experience. For some reason it was vital that I forcefully made myself misfit from the team activity.

Makeup applied, I biked through the neighborhood on my Kuwahara BMX and cut across the field to the team running drills. I felt oddly protected as I rode up the chalked sidelines and stopped near my coach. I sat on my bike looking at all the normal teammates running drills and explained to the coach that I wasn't having fun, and while he was understanding and visibly disappointed, he was also incapable of hiding a distracted, puzzled expression. It wasn't until years later that I thought about it and realized most people don't apply Starman stage makeup to quit something, but, at the time, it felt perfectly normal to me.

4

Corn Maze of Conformity

We are told that schools are places to educate us, prepare us for "real life," build the foundation for success. But, as we've just explored, the experience for a misfit often betrays another, perhaps accidental or unconscious, motive built into the design: conformity.

Certain misfits have an instant, almost spiritually allergic reaction to the entire concept. World champion skateboarder Tony Hawk required limited exposure to an educational institution before instigating such a violent reaction that he was quickly expelled from preschool. Kindergarten didn't start off too well either.

"I was terrified of school," Tony says. Walking into the schoolyard and sizing up the situation, the small and skinny child quickly devised a plan on his first day. "I ran to the fence and was hanging on and wouldn't let go." Fingers locked into the chain-link wire, rejecting sweet cajoling from both parents and teachers, Tony eventually required a careful decoupling of his fingers. "I was terrified of strangers and . . . [starts laughing] a curriculum, because I didn't have one in my life."

But it was evident, even to the hysterical kid, that his reaction put him in the minority. "The size and population was overwhelming," Tony says, but he did notice that he was in the minority, that "most of the kids were going with the flow."

Here's the bizarrely telling thing, though: Tony *loved* learning. One of those kids called "accidents" back in the day, the age gaps between him and his siblings ranged from twelve years to nineteen. His two sisters had already moved out by the time Tony was walking, but they noticed how their young brother had an unusual intensity when focused on learning things that interested him. His older sister Lenore remembers her shock the day she realized her much younger brother had taught himself to read. "When he was four we were driving past Long Beach and there was a big sign for the city and Tony looked out the window and said, 'Look, they have a long beach.'

"He had drive and was pretty much going to do whatever he wanted," Lenore remembers. "Drive and intelligence are a pretty powerful combination. Tony wanted to be able to 'get' things—to be able to read, for example—so he could take care of himself. Once he wanted to do something, like reading or math, he would figure out how to do it. When it was learning something new, then he was interested and attentive and would just put his nose down and not want to be interrupted. But he'd get frustrated a lot—he'd beat himself up if he couldn't do something he was trying for."

Tony's mom told me how disturbed her youngest son became at having to leave an Olympic-sized pool before achieving his goal of swimming an entire length underwater, trying over and over, unable to accept that he might not be able to do it. At that age, Tony rarely looked around himself for comparative placement or a sense of identity. "He really didn't want to ask for help," Lenore says. "He wanted to figure it out himself."

Figuring stuff out for himself, not paying attention to his pace and what others were learning, often unintentionally put Tony out-of-sync when he was inserted into group activities.

By second grade Tony found himself unable to stay focused, fidgeting constantly. "I baffled my teachers. I baffled my parents. I baffled myself," Tony writes in his autobiography. His mom told me how there were various meetings and theories about her son's problems, and the school offered a variety of remedial solutions. Nowadays pharmaceutical intervention would most likely be encouraged, as he already had a loose diagnosis of ADD.

Mrs. Hawk was a special lady who appreciated her son's determination. She earned her doctorate in her sixties and believed it was important for children to question authority. So when a school group assembled to tackle Tony's problem, Mrs. Hawk wasn't afraid to question authority either. She was the only one in the academic assemblage who wondered if it wasn't so much Tony's not fitting into school as school's not fitting Tony, and requested an IQ test.

The weird fidgeting kid scored 144, placing him in the "gifted" category and in the 0.1 percentile of how society defines high intelligence. The dude was bored. The school's reaction reminded me of the Einstein meme with the Robert Kirkman quote: "The thing about smart motherfuckers is that sometimes, they sound like crazy motherfuckers to stupid motherfuckers." Perhaps "crazy" and "stupid" are too harsh for this example, but the quote does convey how outside-the-box, out-of-sync thinking can activate dismissive clamp-down reactions.

Within the learning-industrial complex, a machine supposedly designed to stimulate and recognize intelligence, a kid exceeding expectations caused him to be identified as a problem.* Depending on where the

---

* I have to point out here that in over thirty years of friendship, I've only heard Tony mention his IQ score once, and that was when his mom told me the story for his autobiography. Clearly not putting much weight on a test number, Tony made sure to add "whatever that means" when we wrote about the results placing him in the "gifted" category. He often credits persistence, creativity, and an ability to learn from mistakes as ingredients of his success.

ENTER THE THUNDERDOME

misfit is in their journey, harsh overreactions and diagnosis of why-you-ain't-fitting-in arrive in a variety of flavors ranging from soul-crushing to annoying to traumatizing. No wonder misfit childhood exists in a fog of confusion.

When I look back on my time spent in school and examine my failure to fit in, it reminds me of taking my first flight and trying to wrap my little-kid head around the two experiences of airplanes. It really twisted my melon to connect two seemingly diverse realities: How can you be seated comfortably inside a plane going five hundred miles per hour and feel as if you aren't moving while somebody stationary on the ground sees you zoom past in a blur? How can the experience vary so radically depending on where you're situated?

If normal travels within conformity, then it's as if traditional students are *inside* a plane moving them in a way so comfortably that they're unaware of any significant motion. But to people *outside* the aircraft like us? We experience normal as if we're on the tarmac and it's blasting past us with a velocity so disorienting that it leaves us no hope of "getting up to speed."

Over and over, the misfits I talked to for this book reference school as a seminal activator in solidifying the misfit persona. The misfit life enters a different level of intensity when the penalty for nonconformity carries inescapable social weight.

While the failure to get on board with normal as it blows past can crumple self-confidence, a misfit knows that's nowhere near as shitty as it would feel to go along with the crowd. My inner brick thrower staged protests—still does—on the regular, but early on I recognized this was to steer me away from certain directions and pathways. That said, I remained unaware of its steering me *toward* anything. ***Being a misfit is a search to find that thing, that esoteric culture, that finally does fit,*** but at the start, when you are lost in the corn maze of conformity in situations like school, there is often only a repulsion and rejection of activities and identities pushed on you.

"To put it simply," Seneca says, "when you see the popular kids of your grade you think: *Is that what I should be? Is that the highest level of high school life?* But I didn't vibe with these people. We didn't have similar interests. Our paths felt so different."

It's perfectly natural, when meeting this kind of opposition, feeling this kind of angst, to try and mitigate it. "People knew I was kinda weird," Seneca says. "I would pretend to like the same things as other kids just so I could take part and participate. Then I got older and thought, 'What's the point?' I felt empty, that I wasn't being true to myself, and became hyperaware of that. But you try it. I think kids have to try that and decide if they want to put up a mask and be part of general society or if they're better off not doing that."

Luckily, if we're open and aware we can start to take inspiration and strength from more veteran fringe dwellers. A punk transferred into my junior high school—and this was in the late '80s, before the look was sold at mall stores like Hot Topic and when it still drew aggressive profiling consequences. He arrived wearing combat boots, short spiked hair, a leather jacket painted with hand-drawn logos and statements, and adorned with The Exploited, SNFU, and D.O.A. patches. Just by being who he was, immediately instigated aggressive pushback from the ruling nobility of school.

The preppies and jocks, two groups heavily invested in the school status quo, felt so threatened that they instinctively made plans to defend the old social order. It was like watching a wildlife documentary to see this situation go down from a distance, how the law of the land automatically moved the players into conflict. The new teenager's isolation was instant and brutal, but as a punker he seemed used to it, new kid or not.

Nobody else looked like that in the whole school, yet he walked with his head high, no shame and no looking away when people stared. The early punk scene made it clear that the culture was about challenging the status quo, and he had solidified into that identity. But he did it by being aggressively different, never targeting anybody or even making comments on other people's choices. His own bold choices were enough to provoke an overreaction by the status quo.

He was in my homeroom, and I was skating by this time and reading *Thrasher Magazine* at school. In the late '80s skating was still a loser activity that drew snickers from most of the general population. *Thrasher's* music section always had punk band interviews, and we bonded over that and our similar locations posted up outside of normal. We were both last in, first out. It didn't take long before plans to reestablish the old hallway social order were schemed. One day early morning gossip floated around the hallways that some preppies had tried to ambush the new

punker after school. Word got around that he was apparently well versed in these situations and beat them all up.

He didn't say anything when we sat down in homeroom and talked about Joey Shithead, the lead singer for the punk band D.O.A.—in other words, had a typical conversation. In one way, he had toppled the status quo, but it meant absolutely nothing to him.

Witnessing offense taken by the normal population over a person daring to be different was a prejudice I was used to, but watching it escalate into physical violence was a shock. It seemed oddly impersonal, like two opposing soldiers dutifully trying to kill each other because they wear different nations' uniforms. Except the new punker hadn't declared war—he'd just split from the system, and that was enough to activate a primal response. The impulse to take him out seemed more about sending a message, making an example of what happens to outliers in order to establish social hierarchy.

MARK MOTHERSBAUGH "I was always the littlest kid at school and had a 'kick me' sign permanently attached to me. When you're a kid there's a whole Lord of the Flies thing that goes on, and all the genetically perfect people practiced it on me. They see you and think: *He's different.* I didn't try to be a lightning rod for hostility, it just turned out to be that way. I saw these high school kids that were all tough and masculine and my legs were skinny so I wore two pairs of pants and two pairs of socks to look bigger.

"When I was twelve, I saw the Beatles on TV, and they

looked nothing like anybody in my area, totally alien, and they sounded different. The reaction from people at school was 'Something is wrong with them.' They thought the Beatles were a challenge. In those days, they mostly played country and western on the radio in Akron, Ohio. That was the music I got my ass kicked to so I never liked it. The ruling power kids hated the Beatles, thought they looked 'faggy,' while I thought it was amazing that they combed their hair down instead of back.

"I started to comb my hair down. I was in my own dreamworld, but everybody else combed their hair back and didn't think I should be allowed to comb my hair down. My gym teacher would put two fingers above the top of my glasses and if my hair touched his fingers, he'd paddle me and force me to walk to the barbershop for a haircut.

"More than once students held me down and cut my hair, once taking a straight razor and cutting the front down to the scalp so my hair in the back was normal but the hair up front was totally gone. I sound like a total loser not to have figured out how to solve this stuff. I tried to conform but I wasn't capable. I hated school—kindergarten through twelfth grade. My mom remembers me waking up at night screaming, having horrible dreams about it. My dad would tell me to punch them back. I was embarrassed because I couldn't do what my dad was asking. I was too wimpy."

Let's pump the brakes for a sec. Fast-forward some skips and peep the scene at the end where all us weirdos dig up the treasure. Happy misfit stories always end with the person finding acceptance of their good old outcast self, by settling into life with misfit passions aglow or maybe enjoying how they and other misfits changed the world around them. Just in case this book has started to read like a steaming pile of bummer—all the people in this book, a hundred percent of all my nonconformist friends, have arrived at a place where they only have gratitude for whatever it is within them that causes them to overshoot normal.

Gift them a spell that could magically remove all the painful awkward moments of misfitting? I can't imagine one of them disappearing what they now appreciate as very precious and intense building material. For the outcast who completes the misfit journey, there can be a peculiar gratitude and heaps of dark humor for the struggle that might not make sense to most people satisfied with conforming. It is an exciting, scary, hilarious, lonely, creative, draining, joyful, bonding, uncertain, painful, invigorating wild ride to arrive at that point of thankfulness. All right, that's it. Just want to make sure that it's clear that all this trauma dumping is for a constructive reason.

Even when a misfit does fit in with something traditional, it's rarely a completely clean snap into place with all the other pieces—it's more like the jigsaw piece that looks like it should fit, *almost* fits, but you try to squish it in anyway. "I was a cheerleader, which was a pretty normie thing to do," Michelle says. "I was always trying really hard to fit in with the rest of the girls. But in junior high and high school I always felt like the dirty one, the one that had dirt under her nails. I was always forgetting my socks. I usually wasn't prepared. Sometimes I was benched."

"I was a jock and played sports, but I had long hair," says Dr. Jon

Freeman, who muddled the traditional high school identity process before opening The Brooklyn Strategist, a successful board game shop and enrichment program. Even though he could earn a spot on the sports team, play in a band, geek out with the best of Dungeons & Dragons players, Dr. Jon was in misalignment, and therein lies the rub. "I played in the band and all my friends hung out in the high school smoking section, but the jocks weren't allowed in there. At one point the football team was a day away from pinning me down and cutting my hair off."

The two worlds eventually headed into inevitable conflict—a scheduling conflict. "I had to miss *one* football practice because I had a gig booked, and I let them know in advance." The coaches, overjoyed at one of their players' expanding success off the field, congratulated Dr. Jon and asked many questions offering vast encouragement for his creative and unique life.

Yeah, right.

"They said, 'You have to choose one or the other, and you're off the team if you go.'" Dr. Jon was quickly schooled in how school identity worked. "What a horrible thing to make a high school kid choose between versus trying to find a way to work it all out."

As is often the case, even if you "make the team" of a traditional activity, you find yourself crashing into inflexible standards and practices put in place to curb curious exploration that might undermine the system.* Nontraditional expressions that have no logical bearing on the activity

---

* Some misfits sneak in under the wire. I helped a Super Bowl MVP, infamous for an unconventional counterculture approach to life, with his autobiography. When the NFL mandated clean-shaven faces for all players, he rocked a Fu Manchu mustache and went to war against other rules, even temporarily quitting the league the season after winning the Super Bowl. There are other examples of nonconformists upsetting traditional sports, like the pro baseball player called Spaceman and his peer who pitched a perfect game tripping on acid.

are still closely monitored for anything "weird." Even when a freethinker gets through the traditionalists' guards, it's only a matter of time before divergent goals begin pulling in different directions, demanding a correction from the established framework, often an overcorrection like "teammates" threatening to cut Dr. Jon's hair.

No future

At their most damaging, conformists retool school as the most reliable divining tool available to forecast a child's future. That very public scoreboard illuminating GPAs, varsity team placement, letters on jackets, honor societies, SAT scores, acceptance letters, legacy applications, and homecoming royalty encourages a tidal conformity. When I overhear normal parents ask each other about their normal teenagers, the answer is often delivered as a verbal spreadsheet, with the offspring's categorical placement in some of the aforementioned indicators like a box score.

If your unconventional life puts up points on a different scoreboard altogether, then you'll notice the doomsday siren that authority will sound. The alarm, loud and shrill in order to induce panic in everyone within hearing distance, sends a message: Consider this an official disinvitation to the glorious future that awaits others who follow instructions. Your life will suck and you'll have nobody to blame but yourself. Deviate at your own risk.

And if you misfit, chances are that this social alarm not only alerts you to misdeeds but simultaneously disconnects you from the mainstream. "I never looked to authority figures, I never looked to my parents for compliments," Stacy says.

Never mind compliments—what do you do when the authority *ap-*

proves the disconnect? One time a gang of fellow students ambushed Mark and dragged him into the showers, drenching him like a wet dog before forcibly combing his hair back and parading him around the common area, where other students gathered. They held him on their shoulders yelling, "See? Mothersbaugh has a forehead!"

As Mark was dragged into the showers against his will, divergent hairstyle about to be corrected, the jock bullies passed the school coach with their struggling victim. Mark, seeing an authority figure, pleaded for help. The coach took stock of the situation before laying the blame: "Mothersbaugh, you bring it on yourself."

As any misfit knows, depending on the emotional maturity of the authority figures, a tinge of mass hysteria can make guardians of the status quo overreact and view people not compliant as threats. John Lydon, aka Johnny Rotten, the singer of the *Sex Pistols* who gave a voice to rejects worldwide as a punk pioneer, suffered a debilitating battle with meningitis as a child that put him in a coma, erased memory, and left him with an intense wide-eyed stare and curved spine.

Despite his missed education, he was a passionate bookworm who spent hours in the library reading far above his grade level. But his rebelliousness and independence led a teacher at his Catholic school to call him Dummy Dum Dum, and the nickname stuck. "From the boy who could read and write at four, to Dummy Dum Dum," Lydon writes in his autobiography, *Anger Is an Energy*. "It was a real challenge to break through that, but I did . . . Those fuck-arse hateful nuns made life punishing, so I educated myself."

For misfits, perhaps the cruelest aspect of school is when the people supposedly tasked with bringing out the best, helping students thrive, do the opposite. "I was in the back of my art class looking at subway art," recalls Sacha Jenkins. "For some reason the teacher thought I was going to be a troublemaker, so he said, 'Look, man, I think graffiti is cool. You

can look at this book all you want, draw—just don't give me a hard time and I'll pass you.'"

The snap judgment, the "lost cause" social placement based upon how Sacha looked and his interests, quickly shoved him to the outside by the powers that be. WTF—Sacha wasn't worth the effort to do what that art teacher's actual job was, which seems like it would be to inspire and educate? What, Sacha wouldn't benefit, maybe wouldn't relate to classical art training? There was something about the young black kid interested in street art that dismissed him from the effort? "I gave him *no* reason to tell me not to give him a hard time."

Teachers continued to make snap judgments about Sacha throughout his scholastic experience. "Me and Nas went to the same junior high school and we had guidance counselors and they each independently told us that we should go to vocational school. There's nothing wrong with vocational school, but Nas's father is a well-seasoned, world-traveled musician who is extremely intelligent, but they just happened to live in the projects. My mom was a painter. My dad was a filmmaker. Nas had access to arts and culture and understood it at a young age, that's why he is who he is, but we were being prepared to serve."

Tony also has an equally absurd story, one displaying how fanatical conformist thinking can distort reality for the indoctrinated. His high school's careers class was taught by a jock-favoring coach back when skateboarding was looked down on as a degenerate, gateway activity. Tony, having previously transferred to this school to avoid bullying, was already a three-time world champion. But school is school, even in 1980s coastal San Diego, and this coach enthusiastically backed traditional hallway hierarchy while displaying disdain for divergent kids with strange haircuts who rode toys.

One project had students chart a graph of their skills and the monetary rewards for them, the point being to guide students into "successful" careers. "When you looked at the list of jobs, skateboarding wasn't on the graph, obviously," Tony says. The project was simple enough that Tony worked ahead on his own as the teacher explained it to the class, step-by-step. Tony made a mistake, corrected it, and went on.

The teacher walked the classroom and noticed Tony out of sync, already ahead. Tony wasn't in class as often as his classmates because most professional contests required that he miss a Friday to fly to events. His tardy slips increased, and he admits that it was harder to get up in the morning after he bought his own house as a senior. A student with his own house and car, paid to travel the world, the seventeen-year-old was technically already incredibly successful by the measure of the current project. This mattered not. He wasn't doing it the normal way.

In his autobiography, Tony writes how the teacher "announced to the class that I was never going to succeed . . . if I couldn't follow instructions and work within a group . . . he continued to yell at me, telling me how I wasn't going to go anywhere in life by defying authority and that my future looked pretty bleak if I continued on my path of disobedience."

What was the real lesson being taught in that class?

While school may fail to hammer the square peg through the round hole, it can hammer home the defining moment when you realize even *faking* normal is out of reach. "I remember thinking, *I am never going to be normal,*" Mark says, explaining how his failed attempts to conform became increasingly absurd before he came to accept his misfit status. "I started wearing a suit and a tie to school. I looked like a teacher and thought maybe it would help me with *them,* at least. It did not help. I wore wing-tip shoes that had a design on the toe and in art class I looked down at my shoes and thought they looked like stupid plain shoes and they'd look better with a pink accent line around the pattern, so I painted them. Of course, this was deemed a 'distraction to other students' and I got detention for that."

Repeated failure to normalize can also draw the opposite punishment, removing identity altogether. Fans around the world rode skateboards and wore shirts branded with Tony's name and screaming hawk skull graphic. "I'd fly to an event and sign autographs and then come home and be a ghost in the hallways," Tony says. "It was weird."

It's no wonder that misfits' parents, aware of the damage a conformist institutional setting can do to the individual spirit, search for alternatives. If you are going to stick your kid with a middle name of "Pirate," you probably have a very different view of conformity, so it's no surprise that Billie Eilish's parents homeschooled her. "Not a typical childhood" is a phrase used in a lot of articles about her.

Eilish worked at a ranch and interacted with kids her age who went to school, so she got a whiff of that typical hallway atmosphere. "I was never bullied," she said in a 2020 *Vogue* interview. "It's just a vibe you get. You can tell somebody doesn't like you; of course you can. I had an entire childhood of that, and now it's interesting, because I'll meet fans where I'm like, if I was in class with you when I was eleven, you would have hated me."

Mark was well aware of how many people didn't accept him all through elementary and high school. Technically, being legally blind is a disability, but the infirmity offered him a safe place to visit after his daily school nightmare. "At night I would take off my glasses and everything would turn into a blur. I liked being in that world—there was something that was comforting to me and I loved going back there. I knew that was where I'd go at the end of every day. It was pretty personal and didn't involve other people."

I actually tried to erase myself from high school history. I had no intention of having my graduation picture taken, but my mom wanted one so I agreed, but only if she arranged with the principal and photographer that it wouldn't appear in the yearbook. She was assured it would not be used, which of course turned out not to be the case.

Tony, like every misfit I knew at school, subscribed to the last-in, first-out scholastic battle plan. "After tenth grade, I just dissociated with school, pulled away from everyone," he says. "I didn't identify with them anymore. I didn't feel like I had much in common with them. I just went through the motions of getting my school done at that point. Going to school was an obligation to get through because it was expected of me."

What about those celebrated scholastic rites of passage?

"Yeah, I didn't go to prom," Tony says. "I didn't go to homecoming. I think that was a common thread to all the skaters of my era."

I didn't have a close friend who went to their prom or a homecoming until I was deep into my twenties and met my wife . . . and her date never showed so she wrote his name on a paper pie plate for the group photo. Going MIA for scholastic pageantry was such a given that the question never entered our conversations. It would have made as much sense as asking if I'd ever stuck a pointed stick in my eyeball. "Forget prom—I only went to my graduation because it meant something to my parents," Tony says. "It was walk on stage, get my diploma, and walk right off the stage to my car in the parking lot."

As a senior I was skateboarding when I saw a bunch of students dressed up and going into a hall across the street. Recognizing many of them, I turned to my non–school friend Teen.* "I think that's my prom or something." We stopped skating and looked at the long line of my

---

* A nickname earned when he was told "Get out of the way, kid!" around his thirteenth birthday. Teen protested: "I'm not a kid—I'm a teenager!" FYI: He's still called Teen as a very grown adult.

classmates in fancy dress for a minute as if we were watching a nature program about animals in the Serengeti. We didn't say anything. There was no anger or second-guessing or mocking quips, only a clean-cut sense of disconnection. Then Teen and I turned, dropped our boards, and continued skating the ledge across the street from the event.

Mark returned to Ohio after DEVO had released a popular album celebrated for announcing a new musical style soon to be called "alternative." He sang to sold-out stadiums around the world and his band was watched by the entire country when they were featured on *Saturday Night Live*. The world had changed.

Mark unexpectedly ran into the coach from his high school, the same one who said the musician brought his abuse on himself. "He had hair longer than I had when he used to punish me," Mark remembers. "I said, 'You used to punish me for having hair shorter than you have now.' The coach threw his arms up and said, 'That's the way it was,' and just laughed."

When I asked older misfits, ones now celebrated for a uniqueness that made them targets at school, if they felt any validation after finding a level of mainstream-approved success, they did not respond as one might expect. There were no bursts of anger, tales of revenge, or righteous basking in the glow that can accompany an upgrade in mainstream social status. Every one of them shifted the focus to what they learned through their hardships, and emphasized the message to **hold on to your misfit, and find a way to stay true until you find a scene and/or make a scene where you feel a part of something.**

ENTER THE THUNDERDOME

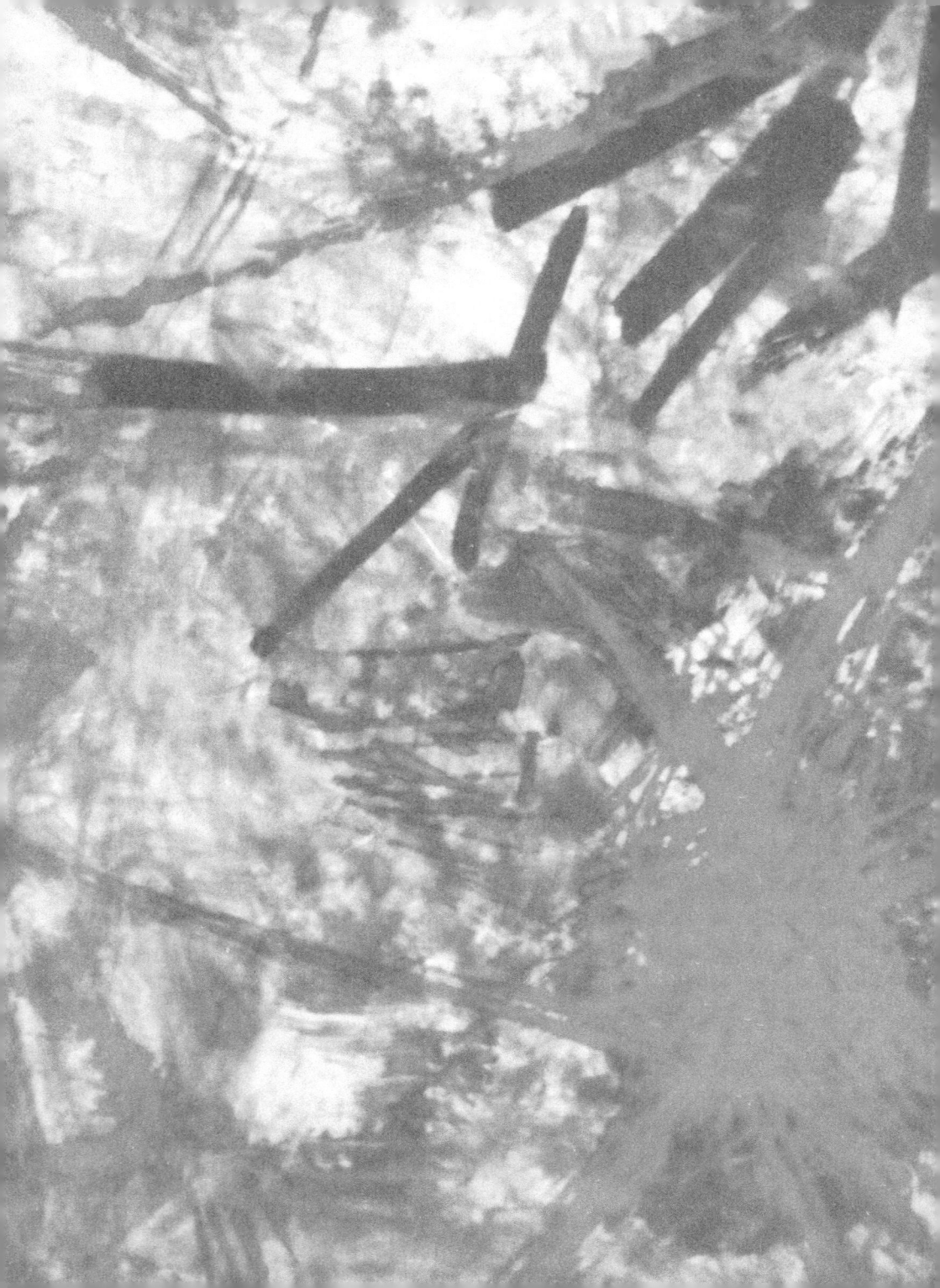

THREE

WINNING BY LOSING

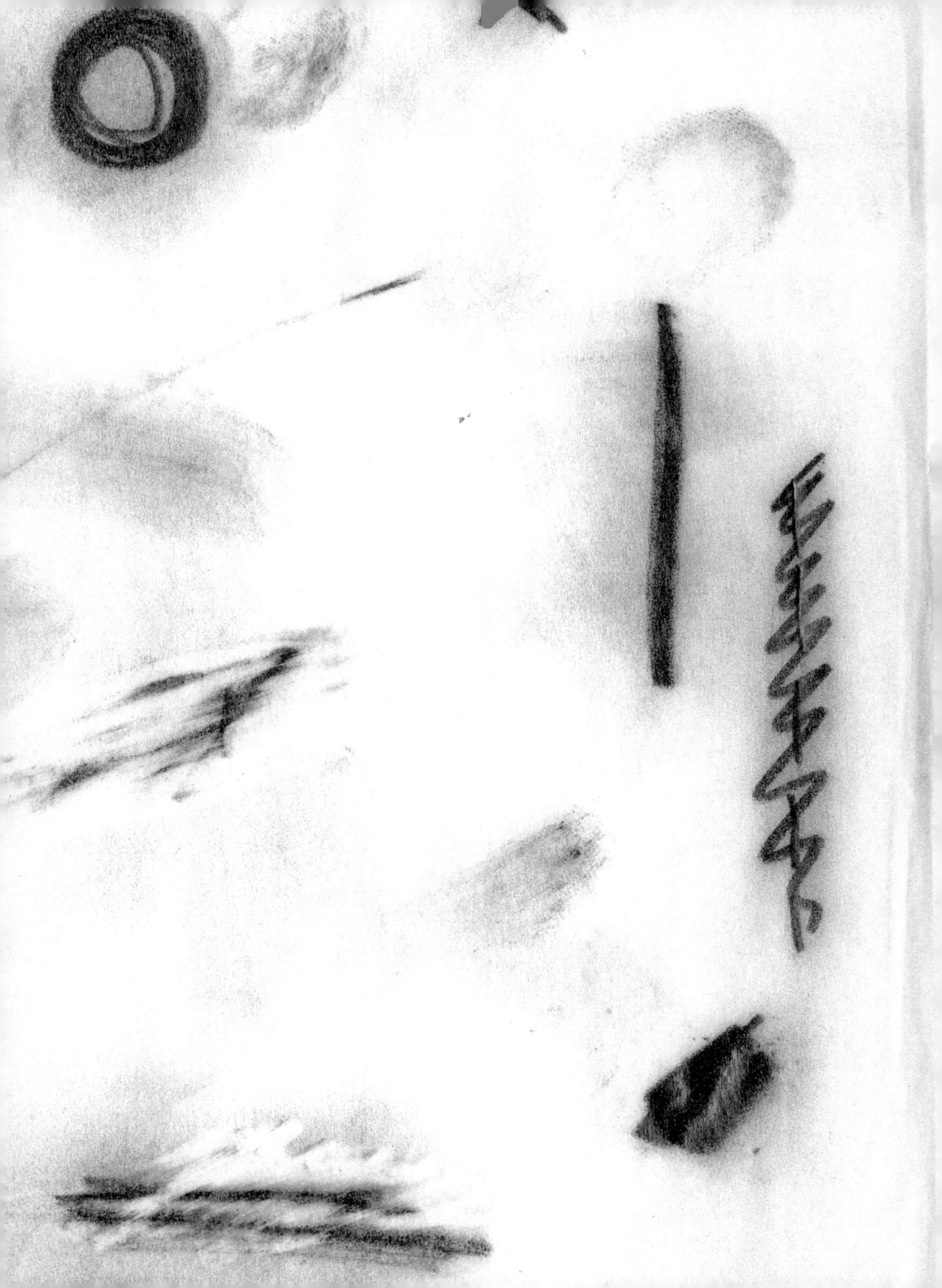

5

Finding the Right Puzzle Box

*C*ongratulations. *At this point in the journey you've lost the fight. You realize you are not normal and stop fighting it.*

When a misfit finally stops trying to contort themselves into an accepted traditional shape, it can feel like a catastrophic failure. Fear is a prime motivator and nobody wants to spend their lives alone. **The part of us that wants to belong at all costs argues mightily before we take it behind the shed to put it down.** No sentient being evolves to enjoy giving up, especially when the stakes are this high. But there comes a time when the misfit realizes they are incapable of putting on masks anymore.

Okay, time to drop a cheat code. What feels like a structural collapse of identity for socially askew individuals is not only necessary but essentially an act of blind conviction. There is no concept of what happens next—all you know is that you're done with this way of life. This is not going to present as a choice made freely, but more like a harsh dunk in paint remover, leaving you stripped down, undecorated, and incredibly vulnerable. The ability to self-bullshit is over, and it hurts, but it's a necessary threshold that none of us would go through willingly.

"All of that early rejection really taught me to think for myself," Stacy says. "It was incredibly great training. It helped me in times of my life when I had done things that were new, and I could sustain long periods without getting any understanding from anybody else. That is really hard. When you are doing something in life and it maybe hasn't been done before, it's a very insecure time, because you don't know what the outcome is and you desperately want feedback, but you don't get it because it's not ready for feedback to be had for it yet. My upbringing was a schooling in how to be an individual without needing support from anybody else."

We're nonconformists, so naturally we're all going to cross trail markers at different times in our lives. I know people who arrived at this point of no return in elementary school, a lot in high school, and some much later in life when their hair was already gray. Personally, I was on the edge of teendom when I experienced this reckoning, old enough to conceptualize the consequence of a life beyond the fringe. **I couldn't shake the feeling that being a misfit was still somehow *my fault,*** that it was *my choice* to quit trying to fit in, which added a rancidness to the defeat. There was an evacuation of self, some spiritual food poisoning blowing sustenance out both ends until the only thing left was a tormented husk.

Powerless to stop failure from filling this new emptiness, I could feel desolation extinguishing any sense of who I thought I was. As is always the case, the unknown is what really juices fear, and I didn't know who or what I was going to be on the other side of this defeat. The only assurance was that it wasn't going to be normal.

The imagined devastation was so intense that I steeled myself for a life without contact, posted up alone on the wrong side of an impenetrable glassed-off barrier. Imprisoned to watch life experiences in real life but with as much contact as if viewing reruns on TV.

Corny? Overblown? Drama queen?

Guilty of all of the above.

Regardless, at that transitional point in my life the fear of not knowing who I was, plus sitting by myself outside the box everyone else was in, stoked a fear real enough to cliff-drop me into an existential crisis.

But as any seasoned misfit or insufferable poet will tell you: You need to get lost to find yourself. Once the illusionary "normal" self is discarded, a new form of wandering comes into play. Mall directories are no help once you stop shopping for processed experiences, so you exit the stale air of the enclosed emporium center for the wilderness. You don't know what you are looking for, but you're now sure about what you are *NOT* looking for.

"I was feeling that the world of South Carolina preppiness and sports is not where I was going to fit in," says street artist Shepard Fairey, the man behind the popular international OBEY brand, admitting that there was no directional sense. "There wasn't any sophisticated articulation of what I was looking for—it was all gut feeling."

I didn't know who I was or what I was looking for when I walked into a movie theater as a thirteen-year-old to watch Michael J. Fox in *Back to the Future*. But I was in the right state to be found.

I still don't quite know what happened.

Marty McFly, the movie's main character, is a loser, constantly harassed by authority figures who call him a "slacker." In the film there are a couple of shots where McFly rides a skateboard on his way to school and another scene where he escapes bullies by improvising a skateboard from a homemade applebox scooter after being zapped back to the 1950s.

I'd never fired a neuron in the direction of a skateboard when I went into the movie theater, but upon exiting thoughts, emotions, and imagination were resettling into a new pattern that I had no conscious control over. An internal switch hidden deep in the shadowy area of my psyche had flipped and a reset was in motion. Earlier I compared the misfit feeling to being a magnet that repulsed other magnets and now, for the first time in my life, it felt as if the polarity had flipped and things inside were snapping together with alarming assurance.

The most discombobulating feeling was how this interior movement happened with a shockingly unfamiliar sense of confidence. I wasn't deciding if I liked skateboarding—that was already firmly decided at some point in time and space hidden from my consciousness. This was a metaphysical change as I experienced destruction and creation in a single action.

It was like living your life with one of your five senses disconnected and then suddenly feeling it get plugged into yourself—it's an unrelatable sensation, yet at the same time as you experience it, it is transfiguring your perception of the outer world. Those minimal skateboard scenes in a movie made me understand how Victor Frankenstein's creature must have felt as hijacked lightning delivered electricity into dead tissue, animating an awakened awareness of life.

People might reasonably ask, "Wait a sec—isn't skateboarding popular and accepted? Aren't skaters the cool kids at school? Ain't that Tony Hawk guy rich and famous?" This is *currently* fact, but when McFly debuted on the screen, skateboarding was a persecuted underground subculture. Skate shops were as rare as Bigfoot sightings, with most product being sold in alternative record stores or head shops next to bongs. No X Games or Olympics on TV, zero sponsorship interest from mainstream brands like Nike, and energy drinks were not even a thing yet. There was nary a glimpse in advertising, since, to the general public, skateboarding made you look like a loser. There was a reason why Fox's teenage character in the movie rides a skateboard—it instantly established him as out of sync as well as literally out of time. He's chastised as having "a real atti-

tude problem," repeatedly late for class and targeted by the head authority figure.

Even though skateboarding was unknown to me as I sat in the theater, there was a noticeable sense of calm as I submitted to being maneuvered by an overwhelming urge to skateboard. I had consistently felt pushed and shoved in my life, anger and anxiety inflaming me as I unsuccessfully tried to remain steady, but this was different. I could not tell if I was moving within this chaos or if the chaos moved within me.

Complete passion was churning, and it created a safe space devoid of social matter, instructions, or sense of direction, and instead of making me feel lost, it smashed together an invincible sense of freedom.

Misfits at this point of discovery are actively doing something many people never experience—exploring. The early stages of the misfit cycle make you feel aimless except for a pinball repulsion away from conventional activities. This provides a sense of direction of sorts, even though it probably doesn't register as navigation, at least not until your misfit passion finds you. And, if you can completely drop the urge to conform and remain open and exploring, finding that passion will happen.

It's important to understand how dropping all efforts to conform and becoming a beautiful loser is necessary in order to clear out all the social identity static. Having a clear channel allows for a higher degree of sensitivity, so it makes sense that some of my outcast friends use the word "antenna" often in this context. "That dude has a good antenna." "Gotta keep your antenna up." "They can pick up the faint signals." Clearing out the general population chatter allows the misfit antenna to start picking up complex coded outcast signals, which, for the first time, put you in contact with passions beyond the conformist borderline. If I was sitting in the theater comparing skateboarding to baseball or wondering if people would make fun of me for riding a toy, that odd frequency would not have made it through.

One hallmark that sticks out among my misfit friends and their misfit passions is not the specifics of discovery (those are all over the place, depending on locations and circumstances and era), but how they began receiving stray signals. When that bent antenna is extended, it starts to receive transmissions in all variety of situations. Roger Gastman would create Beyond the Streets, a brand that brings often "illegal" street art and culture into the general population. But as a child, he picked up a pirate signal coming from somebody hired to help him excel in a traditional institution.

"In sixth grade I was in a tutoring program and if you did well they'd give you a token for prizes, and for some reason there was a Twisted Sister *Stay Hungry* cassette tape and I chose it. My tutor said, 'If you like that, you should listen to a bunch of other bands, and he made me a duped tape with Naked Raygun, Mucky Pup, and the Sex Pistols. I liked the music, the image behind it." That led a preteen Roger to go off the conventional map to explore the varied underground expressions in subcultures like graffiti, street photography, and punk.

The antenna works both ways. Roger's tutor picked up his student's misfit signal and sent a rather strong pirate reply that opened up a whole new universe of education and communication.

There is some brutality inherent in the physical process of birth that makes the shock of transitioning to another world paradoxically beautiful. The birth of a misfit is no different. There was a distinct before-and-after demarcation line in reality when I left that movie theater.

Young Ed Templeton was outside his house minding his own business when a pack of wild atypicals rolled down his street. "I saw a group of kids skate by and one of them ollied up the curb," the artist says. "That blew my mind: How the fuck did they get up the curb? These were older kids that I would have been afraid of and I saw them fly up the curb without even trying. I remember thinking: *I want to do that.* That was the seed."

I want to do that.

And now you, a beautiful loser, are present enough to pick up and follow that signal without judgment. "There were dudes that were a little older and I'd see them around and they dressed kinda punk and they skated and they reminded me of the Greasers from the movie *The Outsiders*," Shepard says of the awareness that he was now in control of his identity. "They seemed like a self-possessed, confident gang. Whatever mojo they had gotten somehow . . . I needed some of that."

Mark was safely tucked inside his traditional house nestled inside a traditional community inside a traditional nation when he saw a new band on TV that instantly changed his perception of the world. They looked different, sounded different, acted different. Forget pirate—the difference between what Mark was receiving versus his everyday life was more like getting zapped by an alien transmission.

It activated the same misfit impulse as with Ed: *I want to do that.* Eventually Mark penned the iconic DEVO song "Uncontrollable Urge" describing the process: "Got an urge, got a surge, and it's out of control / Got an urge I wanna purge, 'cause I'm losing control / Uncontrollable urge, I wanna tell you all about it / Got an uncontrollable urge, it makes me scream and shout it."

Sometimes that urge arrives like a slowly rising tide delivering the same beautifully destructive/creative dynamic. "The first time I tic-tac'd around on my friend's skateboard was in 1983," Shepard says. "The reason the skateboard was abandoned at my house was because it had no social currency anymore. My friend left it and I thought, *I'm just going to experiment with it.* That's all it was: curiosity. Pure curiosity. Nothing that would point to it being a literal or metaphorical vehicle to anything useful."

There is no right or wrong way to discover your misfit passion. I was seated in a mainstream movie theater watching popular entertainment when it hit me—nothing edgy or sexy about that set of circumstances. It's the sense of solo exploration that the process activates, the "uncontrollable urge" that ejects you into an alternate world on your own terms and is so immersive that it erases the old anxiety of "not doing it right." All you focus on is dogged pursuit.

It's not by accident that there is so often a sense of play in misfits' activities—it takes us back to our childhood approach of pure unselfconscious discovery. I was given as much guidance on how to climb a tree as I was on how to fall out of it, and I learned how to balance and fall off a skateboard all on my own as well.

STACY PERALTA "What I loved about skateboarding was that I could do it on my own at any time and didn't have to get anyone's approval. There was no infrastructure to it. Skating was an illegitimate activity and everywhere we did it, we were told to leave. It was making noise or people didn't like it or we were not supposed to be there or it was a bother to patrons or we were on school property. When that happens over and over, you either quit or embrace the illegality. And we embraced that. We liked being disliked because we dig what we're doing and we were not going to stop. You tell us not to be here? We're going to either run from the janitor or the police and come back when you're gone and do it anyways because we love doing this.

"I remember one Saturday when I first started skating and I was on a smooth sidewalk and I'm weaving in and out of people and cars are coming into the parking lot, there was a lot of chaos and I was aware that if I hit a crack or a rock I'd be on the sidewalk, and in the middle of all this chaos I felt this incredible sense of stillness. I didn't realize what I was feeling at the time—all I knew was that this was an extraordinary feeling and I hadn't had it on anything else that I'd done in my life. That strange dichotomy of being close to complete chaos and yet at the same time feeling complete stillness inside.

"I found that mastering it was a challenge, because it was all about balancing and the constant need to readjust, readjust, readjust—you're always readjusting

> because you're always getting hit with obstacles. Didn't make any sense. It wasn't until decades later that I was able to articulate what happened that day, the stillness while being confronted with danger at the same time."

Not only does skateboarding arrive sans instructions, but it's unclear how to win or lose with it. The best skateboarders in the world all ride in unique manners, no two doing exactly the same tricks or developing the same style, no fixed metric dictating a "right" way. You've got to figure that out for yourself, which makes the whole activity confusing and therefore threatening for inflexible people seeking security in being told how to win.

And, like any misfit activity, it also introduces an alternative way to live. "We were in our own little world," Tony says about life when people made "Skateboarding Is Not a Crime" stickers. "We were considered nuisances," Tony says. "No one took it seriously, so, yes, there was heckling."

Or worse. I helped skateboarder Rodney Mullen with his autobiography, and when he won the world freestyle championship at age thirteen his traditional father congratulated him by saying, "I'm glad you won, Rod, you've proved all you need to prove—you're the best. Now it's time to stop and concentrate on another sport, something worthwhile, like golf. That's a sport where athletes *really* compete."

But the general public's heckling, bullying, and dismissals hit you differently at this point of discovery. Before, they were indicators of failing when you wanted to fit in, but now your misfit passion has gifted something alien—the actual urge to misfit *intentionally*. This is the realization of how you begin to craft your own identity instead of being forcibly molded into a manufactured one. The inner brick throwers no longer seem to be protesting, now they're encouraging.

The set dressing of conformity collapses all around you and an entirely new world is revealed when you finally *want* to be different.

Skateboarding is not unique among misfit passions. It's not ranked higher, because there is no silly ranking system for outsider activities—they all start at the bottom, thankfully free of outside grading systems and interest. Maybe it's taxidermy that lights your fuse. Knitting clubs. New art styles. Board games. Toy collecting. Queercore. Graffiti. Some crazy new thing most of us can't even imagine yet. Could be aggro underground roller-skating like it was for Michelle. Geek rock. Nerd fashion. Fringe music. Fringe art. Fringe expression. Fringe identity. If you're open to chasing your curiosity wherever it may lead, not judging whether your interest is "worthwhile," then that jack-in-the-box obsession and identity will spring out of you with frightening connectivity at some point.

What is special, what ranks it high for you, is its ability to ambush with an enigmatic sense of connection that makes you feel a part of something in a way you never before experienced. It's the process, not the specifics, that is a shared experience for all misfits and is often collectively recognized.

So, just because skateboarding derailed my life in the most magical way doesn't mean it'll work for anybody else. As two passionate misfit enthusiasts, it took only about three minutes of meeting Michelle for the first time to feel that we were reading diaries to each other, and it mattered not that my skateboarding was not her skateboarding.

"My dad is into skateboarding and my younger sister Loren is into skateboarding and I wasn't into it," Michelle told me. "One weekend when we were kids my dad takes us to this hill because Loren is ready, and we take our skateboards up there. Loren and Dad go down the hill and then I try and I can't stop and I ride into a curb and fall."

Michelle, understandably bummed, and bleeding, was having a hard time pinpointing the joy in this activity. It's not fun *and* it hurts. "My dad was like, 'This is not what this is about. This is about getting up and doing it again. You're bleeding but you're not hurt, you're not crying. We don't have stop.'"

Michelle understood that, yes, she didn't have to stop, but philosophical ruminations over free will aside, she hated everything about the experience and told her dad she was going home. "He said, 'Okay, but your sister and I are going to stay out here. Bye.'"

Michelle walked home, and of course by the time she reached the front door she understood the awesomeness of skateboarding just like I did in that movie theater . . . or maybe not.

"I just remember thinking, *Fuck skateboarding!*" Michelle says. "*I hate skateboarding! I'm never going to skateboard again!*"

I forgot to ask Michelle if she ever did skateboard again, because we were both laughing so hard, but from what I can tell it doesn't look like she did. She don't need no stinkin' skateboard—she found her own thing. "My parents set up a sixth birthday party at a roller-skating rink," Michelle told me. "I remember putting the roller skates on. When I was younger I would really obsess over death. At night I'd fall asleep thinking, *We never ever ever ever ever ever ever come back?* I tried to comprehend that all the time and then at my birthday party I remember putting on my skates and getting off the wall and thinking, *Oh, this is the feeling! This is where I was before I was here.* It was *that* feeling. It felt SO at home. This world is *not* at home and how I'm feeling right now is where I used to be."

Experiences like that will not be found in a box.

6

Illicit Power Surge

After a lifetime of dead inputs, it is impossible to brace oneself for the channeled power of a misfit passion connecting for the first time.

"Music gave me a goal and a focus for the first time," Mark says of the power of music to formulate an escape. "I was going to be in a band and I ignored the bands I didn't like so I knew it wasn't going to be like one of those. I had something to think about and try. I'd get a 45 of the Doors, and the song 'Light My Fire' had an organ introduction. I'd play it slow on the record player and learn to play it. I felt different. I drew pictures of stages, musicians, made fake music concert posters."

For people accustomed to being asked to leave the party, it makes all the difference when you split on your own with somewhere to go. A misfit passion provides a destination, and that changes the entire power dynamics of conventional rejection. "I went into a fantasy world," Mark says, "and did artwork all day and learned music and looked for people to be in a band with."

The old world that Mark had, at one point, tried so hard to fit into? "I look at my notebooks from high school. They start off neat with notes and then you see a drawing appear, then the next day there's maybe two heads drawn and then an airplane shooting the math homework. By the end, it's just drawings all over the pages and it'll say 'final quiz tomorrow' but the pages are covered with nothing to do with what I'm supposed to be studying."

"Skating just . . . BAM, a whole new world," Templeton says. Like Ed and most misfits at this point, the gravitational pull from the new misfit passion is so strong that you aren't fully aware of how quickly you're pulling away from the mainstream. "I wasn't thinking too deeply about any of this shit—I was just doing," Sacha says. "There's something about just doing it, there's a fearlessness in that, because I'm too busy doing it to be afraid, too busy doing it to doubt myself."

The best part of the misfit journey at this point is something I will call "misfit faith"—an almost mystical trust that this new outcast passion will help craft a new life and it's not up to me to understand how and why. "There was no career objective at the time, no one to emulate," Tony says about his headfirst charge into skateboarding. "No one had made skateboarding a life career. Some people had small tastes of success and that was great, but there was nothing to aspire to in that sense, and that probably made it better because . . . There was no end goal and that made it more fun because there was no expectation."

"No expectations" is not something that tradition, convention, or conformity promotes. For people pining for security, eager to master rules and ways to win, this level of dizzying unpredictability can be nightmare fuel. For the misfit well aware of where traditional rules and conformist sequencing have led them, this instability becomes a thing of beauty.

It is the engagement demanded from this unpredictability that helps us build a new sense of confidence. As Sacha said earlier, "I'm too busy doing it to be afraid," and this in-the-moment presence trains a lack of fear in us without an awareness of it happening. When you are exploring and in a constant state of discovery, the excitement overwhelms any social programming that can make us anxious or insecure.

Where are you when you have no expectations? Right here, right now. And being in the moment, open to whatever is coming, has a way of evaporating tendencies that encourage steering into specific directions for a sense of control.

As a misfit feeling this present for the first time, there is a growing confidence that blossoms into a type of faith. This faith isn't dependent on anyone else and it's not ego reimaging yourself as a chosen one—it's faith in the process needed to relinquish control of expectations, faith in this new way you have of feeling about yourself. Nobody ever told us how disorientation, lack of security, and trust in a chaos that tears apart existing frameworks can leave you piles of building material—can make you feel alive for the first time.

DR. JON FREEMAN "I got into D&D in the late seventies and that was kind of mind-altering for me, a great experience. It was the first board game that didn't actually have a board. It was a game played in the arena of the mind. I think the mind can be much more creative when there are no constraints of what something is supposed to be or what lines it has to stay within."

FOUR

STATE OF
BECOMING

Heading Underground

ED TEMPLETON "My mom regularly took us to get Thrifty ice cream, and we'd drive past an empty corner lot. It was just a field among the suburbs, and skaters had built two ramps on it. I'd ask my mom to stop and we'd sit in our car eating ice cream and watching the guys skate. I watched it like you'd watch zoo animals, from the safety of my car. They were punks with jean jacket vests with patches and studs. To me, these guys were dangerous and I would never dream of trying to be friends with or even talk to them. They were clearly outside of normal society and I was not. I was just interested in skating with the local neighborhood kids. I never skated that ramp. Never. It was gone by the time I was a sponsored amateur."

Misfit passions have a way of mutating expectations so wildly that it puts you in a "state of becoming," as Bob Dylan once put it. A transformative momentum sweeps you away from your old life and begins to construct an original identity as you adapt to this new reality. There is so much going on that it takes some time to understand how this new you—or perhaps "authentic you" is more accurate—is coming into existence.

Each movement that takes you deeper into your misfit passion serves two purposes—information gathering and confidence building. These two actions blend into a metamorphic process that feels as if it's happening of its own accord.

If you'd stopped thirteen-year-old me—anxious and lacking confidence—before I entered the theater for *Back to the Future* and said that if I chose skateboarding I would have to run from cops and even get tackled and put in headlocks by the boys in blue, become a walking target for empty bottles and worse thrown by strangers, and have school guidance counselors laugh in my face, I would have said no thanks.

I hadn't experienced a passion grand enough to offset great sacrifice and did not have access to the confidence required to invite that kind of abuse. I'd have turned the option off, shut myself down, unaware of the change and joy it would infuse into my life along with those obstacles. Before I sat in that theater seat I was a different person. But *after* that simultaneous moment of destruction and creation in the theater? Whether I wanted to skateboard no longer fit into the question-and-answer paradigm.

A misfit passion connects immediately, but the character development behind it happens gradually, without one's realizing it. The journey into an unknown misfit world starts alone, demanding a certain strength of character. Go play Little League, Pop Warner, join the Girl Scouts or various other traditional youth activities in which a parent walks you up

to the registration table, where they line up with other parents, sign official paperwork, pay a fee, receive a uniform, which automatically makes you a member of the team, perhaps even necessitating name patches or random numbers on the back in order to tell players apart. It's not uncommon for multiple generations to have cycled through the same organization and same procedure.

Complete the process and you are officially on a team. Well, as long as you follow their rules. This is a "normal" activity, and traditionalists understand the expected ways to react when playing, spectating, coaching, or practicing. If not, there is a community of controllers around to correct you.

By contrast, fringe subcultures operate in a more cryptic and chaotic manner. There are scant parentally assisted ways for a newcomer to enter an esoteric subculture and automatically "get on the team." Underground cultures exist outside mainstream radars, which can render entrance points virtually invisible to the more traditional.

There is a reason for the descriptive label of *underground* cultures and *sub*cultures. They are hidden from conventional daylight. Skating was declared illegal in many cities, so "skate rats" scurried around in the shadows to avoid being busted. Alternative culture stores and venues are usually located in out-of-the-way areas. Low-rent underground clubs like CBGB and Cuckoo's Nest were created to host the punk and New Wave music that established, "successful" clubs ignored with prejudice. Basements became de facto headquarters for D&D campaigns. Nirvana's Kurt Cobain chose the word "subversive" to describe Mark's band DEVO for a specific reason.

This "underground" aspect of misfit activities forces you to go on a search once again, but this time with a specific mission in mind. For most of us, this search is the first time we've had to figure out how to make life happen completely on our own. "I told my parents that I

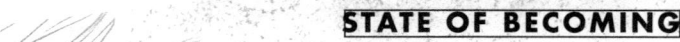

STATE OF BECOMING

wanted a skateboard," Shepard says. "Their only association with skate-boarding was through my dad's head nurse, whose son had dropped out of high school, was doing a lot of drugs, had a mohawk, and was skate-boarding. So they tried to keep me from skating by saying I had to pay for half of a new board. I was fourteen years old and had to raise half the $120, so I mowed lawns and babysat and earned that sixty bucks and then they had to fulfill their side of the bargain."

I love my parents and they never made me feel bad for not fitting in, but they were going to be absolutely zero help in my search to discover what my misfit passion was all about. "There was a ballet teacher in my neighborhood with three kids and she told her kids not to play with me because I was going to waste my whole life riding that skateboard," Stacy remembers. "She was right—there was no such thing as skateboarding back then. It wasn't looked at as a sport or a legitimate activity. I spent three hours a day skateboarding, and there wasn't one time in my life that my parents said, 'Hey, can we come watch you?'"

Not only will normal guides be of no use, parents can even transform into obstacles via stereotypical knee-jerk reactions to anything uncon-ventional. I know many misfits whose parents took away the tools of their outcast passion. One friend's father even extracted an oath from his kid promising that they would quit at a certain age. (FYI: Misfit didn't quit.)

Instantly obsessed with skateboarding after *Back to the Future* and totally clueless, I didn't even know how to start investigating my unconven-tional interest. I had never pursued anything that wasn't readily available. Nobody I knew did the fringe activity, and I mean *nobody*. No friend of a friend, classmate, or distant cousin did anything even remotely related—not that I knew what was related to skating at the time. Back then you had

to look in a phone book called the Yellow Pages for business's numbers and addresses. They sectioned them under various generically labeled groupings. Sports. Tailoring. Music Lessons. Record Stores. Obviously, there wasn't a skateboard section, and it took many dead ends, cross-referencing, and blind guesses before I finally found something relevant.

Luckily, one of the few skateboard shops in Canada at the time, PD's Hot Shop, was not only located in Vancouver, but was roughly only an hour's bike ride away. I traced a map and penciled in the street names so that when I got lost, I'd know what to ask for. As a shy suburban kid with my two-tone beige Sears jacket and mall haircut, I'd never biked this far before, over bridges and through fields, into an unfamiliar part of Vancouver.

Pay phone change in case of emergencies jangling in my pocket, an extra bowl of cereal ingested for fuel, tire pressure checked. But even with all my preparation there was a nervousness around this whole enterprise that I didn't recognize. A fear loomed that not only was I not ready, but that some misstep based on my lack of worthiness would earn me permanent exile from this world I couldn't even comprehend. I was going to screw this up! I'd never felt this texture of fear before. Somehow, this new sensation emitted an awareness of the magnitude in which skateboarding would warp my life, which only ratcheted up the anxiety of blowing it. It does not calm the nerves to understand you have something to lose before you even know what it is.

Stray tall grasses pinched in my wheel's spokes, T-shirt sticky with sweat, face red from the midday ride, I finally arrived at PD's Hot Shop, a tiny store decorated with bold black-and-white signage and crowned with a powerfully aggressive DIY image of a skull that had become the logo for Skull Skates. Clueless to the punk scene at the time, the closest I could compare first seeing the outside of the store to was magically entering a headbanger's school binder.

Known as Rowds in our area, short for rowdy, the long-haired, acid-munching metal heads populated shop classes and were familiar faces in detention with their sleeveless backpatched jean jackets. Wearing their rejection with pride, they drew Iron Maiden's ghoul mascot Eddie and Motorhead's snaggletooth beast on their notebook and tagged Metallica's, Sabbath's, and AC/DC's logos onto walls and lockers. They owned being misfits and glowed in the hallways and designated school smoking areas with a dangerous anti-authority radioactive radiance. The Rowds were the only counterculture vibe I had ever been exposed to at this point.

The awareness of PD's being an actual threshold to cross was so visceral that I stayed out in the parking lot, sitting on the wooden rails and then pacing around, trying to force myself to go inside the small shop.

Later in life, a bunch of us would go cliff jumping in Mexico and we were all psyched in the boat driving to the island and then we climbed the cliffs and looked over and every one of us knew what the other was thinking—*Oh damn . . . how am I going to make myself do this?* I *knew* I was going to jump, but I did not yet know what I was going to do in order to force myself to run to the edge of the cliff and leap. I *knew* I was going to go through the doors of PD's. There was full recognition of how badly I wanted it and how it was going to change me, but at that moment what I needed was behind a wall of fear. Fear of what? What else—the unknown.

I paused at the doorway, looking through the glass for some clue that might make it easier. I knew *nothing* about skateboarding and the guys inside all had short punk flattops and wore mostly black clothing, shirts adorned with skulls, sleeves hacked off, a combination at the time that was a bold enough statement to draw aggressive stares on Vancouver streets. I stared at a crudely contrasted image of a mohawked skull with "HARDCORE" written underneath. My reflection on the glass looked like I'd arrived fresh from a mall portrait studio. I was not hardcore.

I'm *well* aware of how overdramatic this sounds, but the employees at PD's honestly appeared to be ferocious guardians at that moment. I'd never wanted anything in this way before. The hostile reaction I imagined when they discovered that I was just some soft kid trying to fake my way into their scene was enough to give me serious pause. In my mind, their unconventionality was a manifestation of their fierce protectiveness of a beloved subculture.

I didn't care if they liked me—I cared if they could somehow block me from entering the world of my misfit passion. I wasn't aware of any other portal through which to enter my passion. I looked down and saw my hand on the door. Employees must have seen me by now, I thought, and if I turned and ran they'd recognize me the next time. There was no choice but to walk through the door.

A punker behind the counter in his twenties with precision flattop hair and a scab above his eye looked up as I walked through the doorway and greeted me with a friendly nod and a "Hey."

There was no judgment, no riddle to be answered or trial needing to be passed. Or maybe there was and I had passed it. He saw something in my eyes that showed how blown away I was by all the skateboard product. I had never seen that much treasure in my life, and all the strange graphics, colors, smells of the store discombobulated me. I couldn't relate to the explosion of aggressive creativity and nonconformist possibilities, and my expression visibly showed how it was all melting my brain.

Another skater came in and it was obvious that the two guys knew each other by how he asked what the deal was with the employee's face. "So stupid. I was just skating down the street and this dog charges out and bites my leg, totally takes me down."

What the . . . even dogs attack skaters? And they seem, like, crazy casual about it. Scarface turned his attention back to me. "Hey, anything you want to check out?" he asked me as if he didn't know I was a phony. "Got any questions I can help you with?"

I spent forty-five minutes asking many, many questions.

At one point I asked Scarface about "re-actor" pads and the formidable punk softly corrected me by calling them "Rector" in the nicest way I'd ever been corrected. I'd never felt so mind-blown and so at home at the same time. My read on the aggression was correct, but if they sensed you really cared it was aggressively inclusive and aggressively unconventional.

It was total immersion in a new world, one cut off from familiarity and guardrail parents, mandated histories, known rules and laws. It was the first search I'd ever started alone, but immediately after walking through those doors, "alone" was the furthest feeling from my emotional state.

ROGER GASTMAN "I had seen GWAR on some alternative section of MTV News and thought they were incredible—these guys are dressing up like monsters, this is nuts! There was a store called Smash!, which was the punk rock/ metal/buy Dr. Martens store. There was a cross-cultural sense to the store. It was like going into a punk rock store out of a 1980s movie—there's a guy behind the counter with a mohawk, there's a wall of Dr. Martens, a wall of stickers. I wanted it all! None of those things were common at the time. If you needed Manic Panic to dye your hair some crazy color then you went to Smash! to get it. People were not walking around with tattoos everywhere. It was a

lifeline to what we were doing. I went there and got my first GWAR shirt.

"Smash! and Tower Records helped mold what I was interested in. Later on when I did Beyond the Streets art shows in LA, New York, London, Shanghai, Canada, I built an homage to Smash! Records called Trash Records. I want to share that experience with others around the world."

8

The Cultural Wastelands

The misfit doesn't have to be purposely seeking a hidden subculture, sometimes it's all about having the confidence to be open to strange new worlds. Michelle's dad sent her and her sister to a gymnastics camp that shared property with a Rollerblade camp. "I'm thirteen years old and I hurt my wrist in gymnastics and have the whole week off to do nothing." She wandered over to the street skating course, an area with banks and ledges and rails and other objects imitating the real street terrain that skateboarders had adapted to riding.

She began watching campers zigzagging the course at high speeds, doing trick combinations and finally asked a Rollerblader, also injured and on the deck beside her, how it all worked. "Are they thinking . . . do they plan it out before they go in or are they impulsively reacting to the environment? How do they know when somebody else is going to come into their space?" He laughed at Michelle's thought process and asked, "Do you want to do it?"

"Maybe?" Michelle said. "I can roller-skate, but . . ."

"I'll give you these Rollerblades if you can drop in on that ramp" and he pointed to an eight-foot spine.

"I spent all day trying to do it and I got it. I was a size six and he was a size nine but he gave me the Rollerblades." The free Rollerblades did not give Michelle the "this is where I was before I was here" feeling that roller-skating did, so she focused on roller-skating by herself over the following years, wandering around unsuccessfully looking for strays that shared her very specific passion.

Set on following her boyfriend to LA after graduating from college, Michelle read an indie newspaper article on roller derby the week before departure. "There's a picture of these girls and they're flexing and they've got tattoos and they look so cool . . . and they're wearing rollerskates! There was no one like these girls that I had crossed paths with before. What *is* this? I want to fit in. Like, *I* want to do this. I want to be good at this. I did really want to fit in. I couldn't get it out of my head."

The misfit gods were looking out for Michelle because she went to a party that night where a girl on rollerskates was rolling around handing out roller derby flyers. Michelle stopped her and asked if she was in the article. "No, but my friends were."

Michelle spontaneously asks the stranger for life advice, a person whose only connection so far is a love of roller-skating, "I'm moving to California, should I not? Should I stay and do this here because I'm really good at skating. Could I help you?"

"No!" The roller-skating leaflet distributor says. "You should go to LA because they helped us start and they are way better there, so if you're good, you should go there."

Michelle moves to SoCal and wastes no time. "The first thing I did was hit up the LA Derby Dolls and try to get into a practice. I was so nervous and my boyfriend drove me to the parking lot. There are all these girls sitting outside in the parking lot in a circle and my boyfriend was trying to give me the confidence to get out and do this. I don't have tattoos and I'm not trying to overcompensate for my baddassery so when I showed up and

saw a bunch of girls that looked like bikers I was even more nervous. There is one girl with cirrhosis, another one with hairy arms and tattoos. I finally get out of the car and one of them says, "Welcome! Sit down! I'm Razor Slut! You're fresh meat. This is a fresh meat meeting."

Michelle had been in her own world for so long that she totally lacked comparative analytics. She gets in the pack for practice and starts doing 360s both ways and various other maneuvers she thought were normal but quickly made her one of the best in the entire league.

Tony's entrance into his misfit world did not share the same confidence boost as Michelle's. "I went to the skatepark and it was intimidating and overwhelming but so impactful because I saw what was possible firsthand," Tony says.

In a social media post accompanying an awkward photo of a knobby kneed impossibly skinny kid waving self-consciously inside a rundown skatepark arcade, he explained how scary it is to head into the unknown to harvest an identity. "I imagine there are many people feeling a similar sense of self-consciousness today at skateparks across the world; arriving with a new skateboard but with a deep sense of doubt and intimidation that you don't belong, that your gear is too good for your skill level or you're simply not 'good enough.' I knew these fears all too well throughout my youth and I had to push through that discomfort to find a sense of belonging. My advice . . . get out there and try. You might just fall in love with it, and end up finding a unique community that shapes your identity."

Tony straightaway developed a habit. "I started going more regularly," he says, "definitely spending all weekend at the skatepark, trying to go there most days after school."

Michelle remembers the incalculable worth of finding her own place as well. "As a kid, the roller rink was my private place, where I was good. I wasn't good at school, but the rink was *my* place."

As a kid, Sacha moved from the suburbs to gritty New York City, at the time infamous for explosive births of both subcultures and crime. Sacha had a literal doorway representing his threshold crossing into another reality. "I had just moved to inner city Queens next to the projects and my mother told me to go outside and play." Sacha's idea of play, rooted in conventional suburbia, would not survive the transition. "I went outside with a Nerf football but all the people in the park had magic markers, people were dancing—I was all of a sudden thrown into all the stuff that would become Hip Hop."

Sacha was so passionate to this new world that he immediately began layering crisscrossing hip-hop and graffiti subcultures together, eventually traveling outside his neighborhood to bring sibling subcultures back to his block to share with others. "I was also into skateboarding," Sacha says, "and down with hardcore music in New York City. I got my first marker in '79 when I was eight or nine . . . hardcore was 1986. I never fit in anywhere—people who are attracted to graffiti, hardcore, skateboarding are outcasts. They are just kids who are trying to process their identities so graffiti or skateboarding or hip hop or punk or whatever gives you an identity."

When a misfit finds that portal and goes through it to find a connection, when a misfit is *open* for that connection, it is a lesson that shapes lives. Conscious of it or not, misfits begin to learn that crafting an identity is an artform based upon crossing over thresholds inside and outside of ourselves.

STACY PERALTA "Things are going on that we don't even realize. When I open myself up and make myself available to learn new things, when I'm going through the suffering stage, where I'm vulnerable and weak, I really think that that may be the most magical part of the whole experience because I'm opening myself up to life so life can get inside of me. If you think about it, we close ourselves off as we get older, easily, and I don't think that's healthy so it's important to find activities that can pry us open. Life knows more than we do and when we get out of our own way and let life in, it works wonders on us."

FIVE

UNITED BY DYSFUNCTION

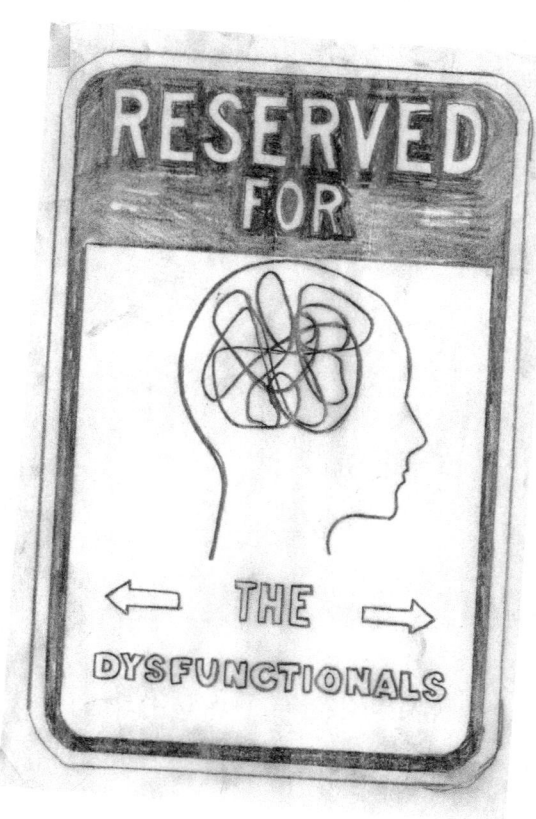

Citizens of Bizarro World

In Superman comics there is a character called Bizarro who is essentially the opposite of the Golden Age superhero. Superman has superpowers, is handsome and buff, possesses straight teeth and glowing skin, speaks proper English with confidence. Bizarro has dead gray skin, directly contrary powers to Superman, and talks in broken opposites, so that when he says "This am great" he really means this shit ain't cool. He lives on a backward planet shaped like a cube called Htrae where welcome mats say "Scram," kids cry when they get straight A's, and junk is treasured. Bizarro was born this way, his brain and body created in direct opposition to the status quo superhero, wired for an alternate POV.

For the misfit who finally locates the entranceway to their misfit passion and makes their way into this otherworld, it feels pretty darn close to crash-landing on Bizarro World. In this new zone, what used to draw derision, invite bullying, and inflict marginalization can be collectively appreciated as superpowers.

"No one is trying to fit in," Michelle says about the most popular participants of her outcast passion. "It is more like, how can I stand out, how can I be different? I'll learn the tricks, but at a certain point, I want to stand out and be different than everyone else."

When you don't fit into mainstream sports, music, fashion, and language, when that has been weaponized against you, it's only natural to create your own style reflecting the differences. Not only that, but boundaries that respectable society has projected as fixed around age, race, gender, income level, and attractiveness prove to be nothing more than chalk lines easily rubbed out by the power of a subculture connection.

TONY HAWK "It was a different demographic, a different type of people drawn to skating—outcasts, nerds, misfits . . . whatever you want to call them. They were not sitting at the cool table at lunch. To be a skater in those days it took being unafraid to do something different and a sense of confidence in doing so even though you were going to get flak for it.

"It took a certain type of person and personality to continue doing it, and what I realized later was that it was people who were very creative with an outside-the-box thinking and their unique approach to life, activity, craft was one that you wouldn't find in anything traditional. I liked that I found a really creative group. I loved the music, that they dressed differently and they all spoke the same language of skate tricks that was indecipherable to nonskaters, and we wanted it that way. You're not invited to the party. We have our own thing over here. It was a whole new world."

When I discovered skateboarding it was such an underground activity that there were probably only a couple hundred skateboard T-shirts worn in all of Canada, and I owned one of them. I had saved up enough money to finally buy a skateboard and studied the aesthetic like an anthropologist, obsessively reading my subculture's magazines and fantasizing about hanging out in the sunny SoCal streets and on ramps alongside pros like Lance Mountain, Tony Hawk, Neil Blender, and Tommy Guerrero.

It was obvious that my underground culture designed shirts to proudly and uniformly scream "Outsider" by being adorned with a mishmash of bright surfer colors, skulls, altered warning signs, graffiti, and dragons. It was clear to harborers of prejudices and participants alike that this was a reject aesthetic. During the first week of junior high I was in the jungle, the nickname for the chaotic area where rows of lockers smashed hundreds of students together, when my misfit radar blipped. Through the frantic interweaving of crisscrossing students, I caught the peripheral flash of a skateboarding skeleton on a yellow shirt and locked onto this unknown kid like The Terminator. Outside of PD's Hot Shop employees, I had never seen another human wear a skateboard shirt in the wild. I closed my locker door, slammed the shackle of my combination lock into the case, and went off in pursuit.

As a child who didn't talk until he was almost three years old and then spoke for a period with a speech impediment, a kid who cried when other people stepped on bugs, cried again when he left his dog to walk to school, cried at spelling tests, a pathological shyness was the best defense I knew of for hair-trigger emotions. I had never walked up to a stranger in my life, but my misfit passion vaporized previous restrictions like nervousness.

I instinctively recognized that this stranger kid and I shared a deep connection, knew something intimate about each other. So, it didn't weird out Ryan when a kid with zits and scabs on his elbows, a rip across his jeans's knee, and a bad homemade hair chop and dye job walked up to him and cut through the superfluous expected politeness.

"You skateboard?"

He looked at me, scanned my shoe and saw the ollie hole in my Chuck Taylors and could tell that I skated, smiled and nodded, "Yeah."

And that was it. I didn't know what grade he was in, if he lived in a shack, if he was considered attractive, if he was cool or rich or scored straight A's—all I needed to know was that he skated. We quickly made plans to skateboard after school. In Bizarro World it is this easy to fit in. All you need is one other person on the same backward planet.

There is a saying that "like attracts like," which explains a lot about the will to conform, but I rarely experienced that type of social gravitational pull in traditional culture. One of the most beautiful aspects of being a puzzle-piece-in-the-wrong-box is that when you connect to your outsider passion—any passion—it gifts the Bizarro potential for attraction. In a way that was unimaginable before, you experience an almost spooky sensation of "unlike attracting unlike" where so many of our irregular edges snap together with other reject pieces.

As the scabs from falling off my skateboard regularly appeared on my elbows, shins, knees, knuckles, face and my wardrobe was infiltrated by strange wares imported from California, I noticed totally different reactions from other outcasts. My dedication to my misfit passion forged a confidence, and when I looked other misaligned people in the eye familial acknowledgments were returned. On the surface we couldn't have appeared as more different—headbangers pulling drags off their smokes with Sabbath backpatches, goths with eye shadow and dyed black hair and torn Cure shirts, punks with Doc Martens and spiked hair, hip-hop

heads with Kangol hats, graf artists with paint drops on their shoes—but by committing to the peripheral we recognized a collective residence in the same territory.

Subcultures organically create coded ways to recognize each other. "There's certainly a kinship in having artistic aspirations," Sacha says. "I think if people have aspirations with style they will recognize someone else who has those aspirations as a point of interest, a way to connect. In the eighties and nineties if you wore Doc Martens a certain way you knew that person was part of a subculture and you could have a conversation with them on the train."

Occasionally, a misfit lifeline is thrown from within the machinery of the mainstream. An art teacher with a bent antenna picked up on Mark's talents and stepped in to take control. Recognizing his singular artistic vision, she helped him apply for an art scholarship to Kent State University. This misfit adult in a position of authority recognized an invincible artistic vision struggling for freedom of expression and felt an obligation to help.

That teacher undoubtedly realized how escaping the confines of a conservative town would expose a new world for Mark where he could decide his own direction. But this was a rescue mission in more ways than one. America had a draft at the time, and if eligible males of a certain age were not enrolled in college, then they were likely to be drafted into active military service in Vietnam. Mark had already had conversations with his brother about what toe to shoot off in order to be ineligible for the draft. He was in danger of being forced to enter one of the world's most conformist institutions.

Kent State allowed Mark to avoid military boot camp, keep his overgrown hair, and experience life where his bull's-eye aura blended in with all other types of targets. "It was a night-and-day difference—I was anonymous," Mark says about attending an artistic school with thousands of people going in different directions instead of hundreds marching lock-step through high school. "Some classes I liked, some were boring, but there were people who were wilder than me—I didn't stick out anymore. I could be whoever I wanted to be."

"That's the beauty of being grown," Seneca says. "You get to choose your own path and you don't have to adhere to these other rules. All during school I felt that I didn't fit in, but when I went to design school, I was like, 'These are my people!' All the things that had been deemed 'not cool' in my childhood were now the focus. It was the first instance in my life where I felt I was really seen."

Mark may not have developed physical calling cards like the identifying footwear destruction of skateboarders, but a misfit's peacock feathers are going to unruffle somehow, sometime. "I fell in love with printmaking," Mark says. "It was empowerment. I'd stay at the school all night working on a print and go home with a new piece of art that I'd created." Art like an astronaut holding a potato or people throwing up in front of the moon. Mark anonymously posted his renegade prints around campus, and what had previously earned abuse now acted as a creative call to arms. "Another student came up to me and asked if I was the guy putting up pictures of astronauts holding potatoes. I said yes. Then I found out that he was the guy teachers in the English department said wrote disgusting stories, and we hit it off."

Misfit expression has a way of turning into pirate transmissions that other askew people pick up once their bent antennas are extended. Notice, though, that there has to be some sort of key, some alternative way of thinking and/or knowledge to understand the encrypted signals. Jerry intuitively decoded Mark's "I'd rather be in space" vibe in the cosmic potato holder print, whereas a conventional person might simply dismiss the unauthorized street art as stupid or "not real art."

If Mark had flexed his drawing skills and printed safe, expected artsy

Pop Art posters, he probably wouldn't have attracted Jerry, who peppered his own communications with a signature weirdness, to the shock of his professors. Instead, Jerry and Mark went full-tilt weirdo and found each other and started DEVO, a band that *The Hollywood Reporter* decreed "were never really a copacetic fit for mainstream American pop culture—too weird, too artsy, too smart, too subversive—but they somehow managed to sneak through for a while."

One of the most surprising aspects of this alternative connective action is how random and happenstance it feels. One cannot simply Google "weirdo friend . . . but, like, you know, my kind of weird" to find a partner in status quo crime. The way misfits pick up each other's signals is as important as the signal. Potatoes and spacemen do not create a naturally assumed intel transmission, but on Bizarro World? This allows for an incredibly complex form of communication. This intricate language is understood so widely because it is rooted in an initial shared pain. All of our journeys, trials, and tribulations add flourishes, but we recognize that our communications are rooted in the hurt of rejection.

ED TEMPLETON "There were some punk guys at middle school. These guys were scary. Ron had a mohawk and would spike it. I watched him get in a fight with someone more conventional and it was scary watching people punch each other in the face. I felt like a complete nerd. I had dreams of becoming a ninja and was a total dork, but when I started skating those punk guys accepted me. Skating was the ticket into their weird world, not that I was even aware of wanting to get into it. I walked into school with a skateboard one day and it was literally,

'Oh, you skate? Come hang out with us.' I suddenly went from nerd to . . . I don't think I thought I was a cool kid, but suddenly I had friends and I wasn't trying to be a ninja."

M y sole skate buddy at the start of junior high, Ryan, had a secret that nobody else cared about—his brother-in-law was Canada's only professional skateboarder at the time and he was going to be at the house on Friday. Naturally, I forced Ryan to invite me over. Kevin Harris was ranked second in the world for freestyle skateboarding, was married and ten years my senior, but, as we know, those differences don't matter on Bizarro World.

Kevin immediately became my best friend, and we skated together that Friday night and almost every night regularly afterward. We shared the same stupid sense of humor, same homemade enthusiasm, same struggle. When we'd retire like two grungy Cinderellas for a post-session Slurpee at 7-Eleven, sweat steaming off our backs as we sat on a curb fantasizing about a world that accepted skateboarding, clothes marked with skidded grime from falling, we were ageless.

Kevin regularly traveled to California for contests and returned with mixtapes of rare exotic alternative music, cassettes given to him by tour-mate and fellow pro Tony Hawk, who never traveled without a fistful—underground bands I had never heard of like the Sisters of Mercy, Stiff Little Fingers, the Pixies, the The, Agent Orange, Youth Brigade, T.S.O.L., Wall of Voodoo, the Vandals, and DEVO.

Before these mixtapes, music had never penetrated very far inside my head. I had bought maybe three albums in my entire life, including an

Alvin and the Chipmunks LP, but "alternative"* music introduced another dimension of that misfit connection, revealing a way to feel that same off-kilter passion through another medium.

"I wanted to get an Agent Orange tape from the moment I heard them in the surf/skate shop," Shepard says, "so I called a bunch of record stores and they said, 'Yeah . . . we don't carry that. We've never even heard of them.' Then I started asking all my new skater friends if they had any Agent Orange and one said, no, but I have *Never Mind the Bollocks, Here's the Sex Pistols*. A few months later, a BMX friend gave me the first Suicidal Tendencies LP. Then I was on a quest."

The punks who adopted Ed at school sketched underground band names and logos on their folders. The kid who had formally planned on an occupation as a ninja asked about the confusing logos. "Next thing I know, he's saying, 'Listen to this' and giving me a cassette tape that had Dead Kennedys and 7 Seconds and all these punk bands on it," Templeton says. "That was an explosion."

New artwork. New activity. New music. New fashion. New expression. Once an outcast starts their search, the new vibe becomes capable of influencing all aspects of life. And these influences open up previously hidden conduits, allowing for other underground streams to cross.

There are so many couples in my life that have seemingly diverse interests, but are together because of these crossed influences. Often, all that is needed is one askew characteristic in common to draw two seemingly very unlikely mates together. I know someone who went to school and lived in the same neighborhood as a girl but didn't "see" her until

* I never heard any fringe participants refer to this type of music as "alternative" at the time. This category label became common only after energetically fringe music began selling enough to attract the attention of mainstream music industry marketing departments.

noticing her at an underground show. So many misfit connections plugged in right there that told them so much about each other. They eventually got married, and still look back in awe over how strong and instantaneous that connection was in that shared misfit space.

TONY HAWK "I identify with my son Spencer in that he chose this very obscure style of something that was already established and made it his own and people started to come around to it. It was a tricky path. There were not a lot of people doing that kind of genre of music, but you could see where it fits and what it relates to and the type of people that are passionate about it and how they created their own scene. He helped to create a scene. I definitely relate to and feel that sense of comradery and sense of exclusivity: We found our thing, and we're coveting it."

Misfit subcultures influencing each other often recognize an unconscious strategy that brings to mind the ancient proverb "The enemy of my enemy is my friend." New York City and the surrounding boroughs is one of the great misfit capitals of the world. The availability of diverse and ultrarich subcultures are in such close quarters that they seemingly draw power from each other. Punk, Pop Art, the Beats, jazz, breakdancing, folk music, gay rights and house music, hip-hop, avant-garde rock, abstract Expressionism, neo-Expressionism, and graffiti are

all wired deeply into the area, feeding off New York's history as a premier freak gathering point.

The Beastie Boys, for example, started as a punk band, but their misfit motivation was so universal that it wasn't deemed necessary to stop and declare a new identity in order to enter a different genre. They simply kneaded that raw energy and self-deprecating humor into hip-hop to make something as honest but much more influential and unique. Then they later released a jazz-funk album.

When Sacha tells me about his childhood move from the suburbs to across the street from the projects, it sounds as if he was dumped into a counterculture blender with a stuck pulse button. "Graffiti was intersecting with hardcore, which was intersecting with skateboarding," he says, adding how hip-hop and tagging were everywhere immediately outside his door. As an observant kid with a face scarred from chicken pox in a new world, the main ingredient of the counterculture glue was glaringly obvious.

"Dysfunction," Sacha says. "Dysfunction and the search for an identity. The people involved were trying to be somebody, and when you're in an environment where you feel that you don't matter, you want to create your own identity that you can own and manipulate. I've come to learn that the white kid who likes heavy metal and has a boombox is the same as the black kid who likes hip-hop and has a boombox. It's the same dude. Obviously, some things behind the scenes are different, things in society, but the base level of what they're interested in is the same."

"That goes to the core of it," Templeton agrees. "Dysfunction comingles with dysfunction pretty well. When you get into that world, suddenly you're immersed with all of these people. Suddenly I, and all the kids I skated with, were listening to punk and found ourselves on the alternative track. Those punk kids were obviously rebelling in some way to be rocking a mohawk at school in 1985, and for me to find skating as a dysfunctional kid was freeing and felt rebellious. I think all the kids who found skating were in that same general position."

Now an internationally acclaimed artist and brand owner with fringe friends from different cultures and countries, Ed recognizes the importance and the universality of the older misfits who culturally adopted and educated him as he perpetuates that cycle himself. *"Oh, you're a fucked-up kid? We can just smell it. Come hang out with us."*

STACY PERALTA "When I was a teenager we had a mail lady who was a hippie—underarm hair, didn't wear a bra. I was skateboarding in front of the fence in front of my house like I did every day, completely lost in my own world, and then I see her not walking toward the house, but toward me. I thought, 'Oh, no . . . not her.' I know what she's going to say: 'When I walk around this block will you please not do that because I'm afraid you're going to hit me.'

"She walks up to me. 'I come and deliver mail and I see you out here doing what you're doing every day and I want to tell you something: What you're doing is really beautiful. You look like a ballet dancer.' She walked away and delivered the mail and I actually thought something was wrong with her. I was so conditioned to believe that what I was doing was degenerate and useless that I actually thought she doesn't know any better, she's just a hippie. She was the first adult to ever compliment me.

"I never looked to authority figures, I never looked to my parents for compliments. There was a beach in Santa Monica called Bay Street and it was an absolute surf scene and I started hanging out there when I was fourteen. My goal was to be respected on that beach, to be somebody who the guys said, 'That guy is a good surfer.' That was all I wanted. It's not that I didn't want praise, I just wanted it from my peer group. I could have cared less if it came from a schoolteacher. I didn't need their approval."

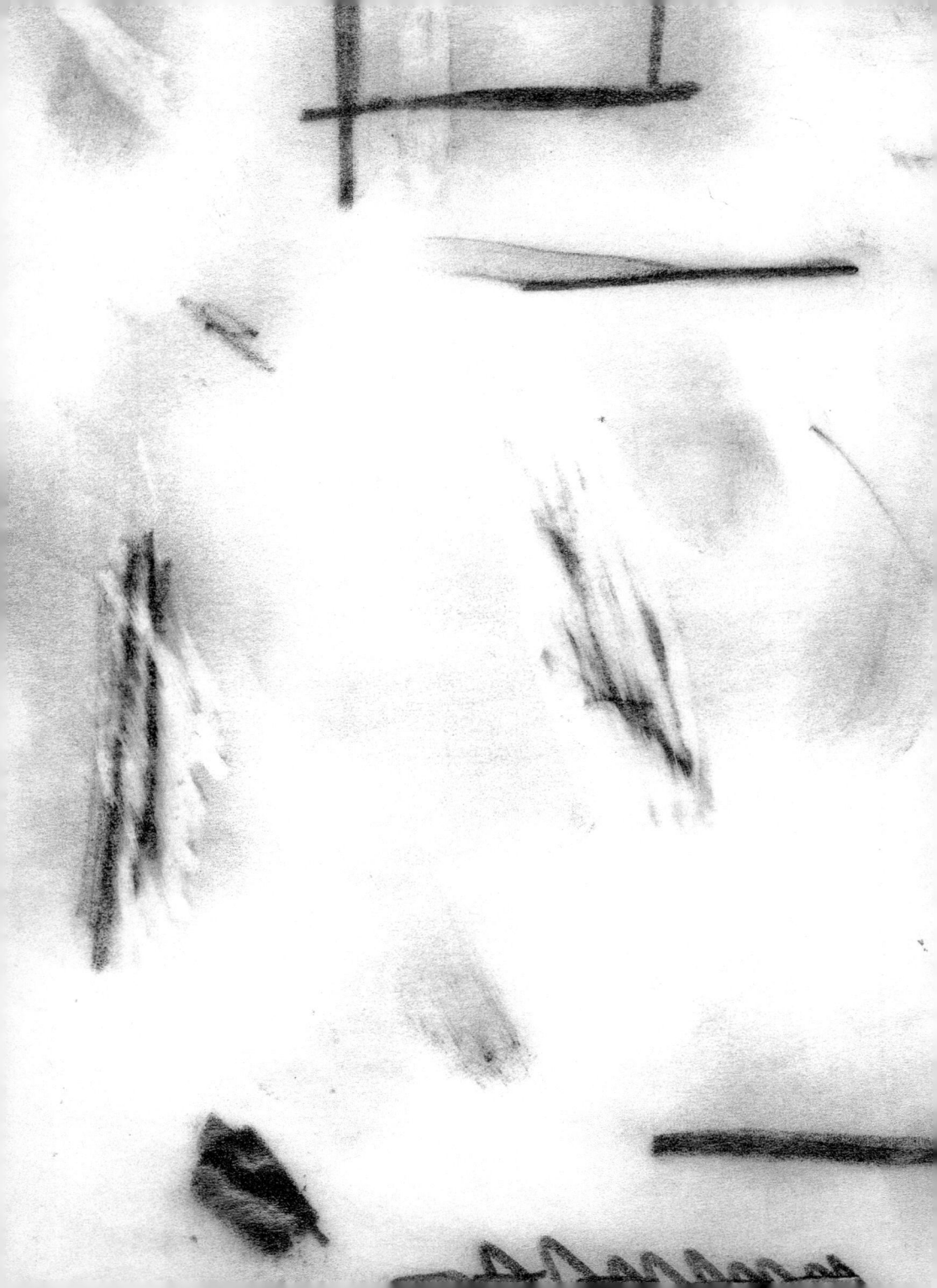

10

Unifying the Kingdom with Style

Before skateboarding derailed my life, I was a plain piece of suburban white toast. I listened to whatever the radio fed me, drew gory fantasy art, played street hockey. I didn't feel that I fit in, but there was no "snag," as Templeton put it to me once, to draw my attention away. You don't know what you don't have in your life, and I can safely say that with everything served up perfectly average, room temperature in all aspects, I had no concept of style in any manner. But then that snag pricked and a misfit passion entered the bloodstream, changing the actions and reactions of body and brain.

While on a family vacation in Oregon, I secured a promise that we could visit a skate shop. I had saved up enough paper-route money to buy my first skateboard and I went into the skate shop and took in the creative chaos of a wall of skateboards with a different objective—to pick one. Today, most everyone is familiar with a skateboard, but as a kid trying to crack the code, my brain was constantly shuffling various stimulations in an effort to make sense of it all. Why are skateboards colorful and artistic but baseball bats aren't adorned with flames and graffiti? Who wouldn't think a tennis racket would pop more with a skull with dreads screened on it?

I scanned the wall of boards and stopped. It was as if I had been slapped, and not in the nice way. The first time I saw C.R. Stecyk III's iconic "Rat Bones" graphic on the bottom of a skateboard deck was the first time I understood the power of art. The kid sent to psychologists by nuns had grown to create a seemingly simple piece of graffiti depicting dead rat heads with crossed bones underneath. This was screened on a Powell-Peralta skateboard deck complete with paint dripping down, as if the artist had hurried to avoid arrest. It destroyed me. **It told me something about myself in a primitive language so atavistic and complete that it resisted translation into anything my conscious mind would unintentionally reduce.** It took all my misaligned experiences up to that point and somehow made sense of them. How? How does somebody do that? I understood the transformative power of art in that moment, a moment that has never ended.

I still get dazed by that artwork, so in order to achieve a better understanding, I asked the man responsible for recognizing C.R. Stecyk III's illegal graffiti as something to put on the bottom of a skateboard. "Here's the thing," Stacy says, "graffiti was not considered an art form back then in the 1980s. It was seen as pure vandalism, and we grew up with that because there was a lot of Hispanic gang culture in Santa Monica and Culver City and they had their own styles. We were always seeing this stuff on walls."

Ah, yes, yet another example of diverse misfit cultures crossing and influencing each other. From the general population's POV, surf rats riding waves in the ocean and Hispanic gangs' landlocked territorial markings could not possibly intersect.

"I remember being at Stecyk's house in the 1970s and his girlfriend said, 'Craig thinks graffiti is artwork.' I'd never heard that before. It troubled me, because it was a concept that I couldn't get my head around. He was airbrushing a lot of surfboards and there was an ele-

ment of that in his style, blending into his own work. Later he did do graffiti artwork, but you only saw Craig's work on out-of-the-way places, very specific places like The Cove.* Craig wasn't spraying stuff around town—he did it specifically around the surf culture. He did the pig and crossbones and the rat and crossbones that we later called the 'Vato Rat.'"

Stacy experienced the dysfunctional impact of these crossed subcultures and understood exactly what this symbol represented. "Imagine a kid in a port somewhere and the first time he saw a pirate ship pull up with a skull-and-crossbones flag? Imagine how many kids saw that and went out of their minds?"

Well, misfit kids at least.

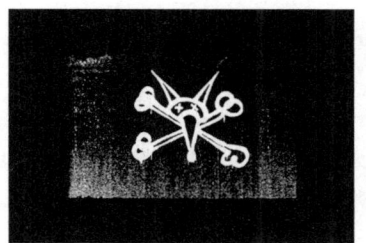

ART 045
FPO

"It is the perfect graphic—it explains the pirate lifestyle perfectly. The 'Rat Bones' is the same thing—it explains the skater's lifestyle perfectly. Another part of it is that Stecyk left in the drips on the skateboard graphic. That has become very popular in the last ten years in commercial art—to actually see the imperfections—but he did it back then. It was graffiti. It was rough. It was simple. And it was badass-looking."

It was the first time in my life I had ever witnessed . . . no, "felt" is

* The Cove was an area on Santa Monica Beach underneath a burned pier and abandoned amusement park.

the more accurate word—**it was the first time I had *felt* imperfection being celebrated.**

I bought that red "Rat Bones" deck, and that night my family walked over to a very steep hill by the hotel. My dad asked to see what this skateboarding was all about. I made it halfway down before speed wobbles pitched me off and I skipped along the pavement tearing my hip and knee to the bone. My shirt and jeans were ripped and my ribs and knuckles road-rashed. My parents saw how undeterred I was and how I slept with my new skateboard by my bed and never once tried to make me stop. Seeing "Rat Bones" to this day still agitates the same sense of discovery. Having picked it myself, looking at it in my bedroom, and repeatedly drawing the art myself, using it to explore a new counterculture felt like a self-inflicting act of genetic splicing. A crude symbol in the style of illegal graffiti on the bottom of a disenfranchised toy taught me how style, which comes from within, transcends normal labels. And **when we do enough work to rid ourselves of preconceived notions, there is so much out there ready to inspire.**

Experiences like this force a contrast and awareness of the mainstream's habit of pushing off-the-rack styles meant to convey individual expression. You'll notice the culture vultures swoop in once the authentic expression of an underground culture—its style—gains a certain level of popularity. As a misfit who has traveled this far in the journey, you know what a cheat this is—a cheat for the person adopting the style. Authentic style is like a scar in the way that what makes it meaningful is the story behind it. This can be why within subcultures that develop their own sense of style, fake style, an affect by design intending to project an inauthentic vibe, is immediately regulated as a dishonorable crime, an identity lie.

"When I was coming up, yo, you wanted people to know it was *you*,"

Sacha says. "Instantly. You wanted to stand out . . . your signature, the way you write, the way you dress, the way you speak—you wanted to stand out. That mentality is a powerful way of thinking that can even influence you to corporate America if you wanted it to. **This idea of being original and standing out, people recognizing your brand on sight—these are principles that I learned as a combination of all these subcultures.** I've done a few things in my day that I didn't necessarily go to school for, but I did go to school in these subcultures."

When a misfit merges with their passion, enthusiasm allows self-consciousness to become porous, allowing style to ooze through. I was talking to some people playing a Magic: The Gathering game, and it became clear in about three seconds that they all had incredibly diverse styles of playing the imaginative card game that conveyed something about them. One was technical, one was flamboyantly irregular with a wild lopsided approach that either won or lost badly, and one was deceptively low-key. Their style came out in the natural expression of their subculture, in this case showcasing a prioritized ingredient—game strategy.

Somebody outside their culture might have looked at the superficial aspects of their style and seen only players wearing a basic wardrobe and assume they had no style, but within their rich culture each individual's distinct style came blasting through.

What is the activating agent in style? What is it that starts developing when we activate with our misfit passion? "Kids wanting to be number one," Sacha answers. "In the world of graffiti, a graffiti master is labeled a king. 'I'm King of the Four Line.' . . . 'I'm King of the A Train. I've mastered it.' It's a very simple, rudimentary understanding of how politics, legacies, dynasties work. A little kid calling another kid a king because they have the most paintings on the Four Train? That term comes from people wanting to be recognized as the best, number one, and the thing that puts you over the top is having a style that is unique, one that stands out."

"The people who have faced more resistance have a lot more emotion coming into their creativity," Michelle says when asked about the building blocks of style. "They just can't help themselves. The more emotion that is coming out, the wilder the style. Style is not something that can be copied, it is something that comes from within."

I've never witnessed authentic style arrive consciously. It always has an element of mysterious spontaneity with a tone of truth reverberating through it. Truth of character. *How* you do something in misfit culture can be extremely revealing. In baseball nobody cares how you hit a home run—it is the home run and the number on the scoreboard that matters. But in skateboarding how you did a trick makes all the difference, because it conveys an aspect of personality with it, and from that a connection. How Stecyk spray-painted the Vato Rat mattered. How Seneca designed an oversized third eyeball mattered.

Like a single bar on your phone, weak style emits a weak signal and a broken connection, whereas a strong style is four full bars and clear communication. Powerful natural style hits you in a very unconventional way—it doesn't make you want to copy it, it feeds an inspiration to go deeper and experiment with your own.

Many truly gifted misfits I know are inspired by diverse styles that have nothing to do with their passion. I've heard skaters talk about grinding a handrail like a jazz musician, photographers talk of framing like painters, musicians riffing on antiquated art movements.

But style can also be a form of self-correction when it grows to a self-indulgent size within a subculture. Misfit style often begins as a reaction. Tradition mandates that a conformist type of haircut is "respectful"—then I'll dye and chop an argument atop my head to challenge that assumption. You say this isn't music—I'll slice and dice old tunes into a new form of sonic expression. You say this isn't a true sport—fine, we'll build it as an expressive physical artform. But often a

culture moves beyond what it was reacting to as it evolves, and a calci-fied style becomes a de facto "rule." Luckily, style has its own fail-safe for that situation.

Michelle reminds me that style is often expressed via pushback to *any* restrictive force, not just misfit vs conformity. "Some of the community will be talking about 'rules' of style and then the more stylish ones will bristle at that," she says. "They say, 'Don't tell me what to do!' Then they'll deliberately add a flourish to what was supposedly forbidden. They'll take that criticism and make it better for themselves rather than just listening to friends telling them what to do. Style is an extension of our personalities and this is what makes us feel good and there are no [starts laughing] . . . there are no rules in therapy."

SIX

PIRATE UNIVERSITY

Functional Fixedness and Other Disabilities

SHEPARD FAIREY "When you go to art school, it's based on art history, really ruled by white European perspective. If you want to play the game within that then you're pushed to take certain paths, routes, learn techniques. I looked at this system, partially out of defiance and partially out of insecurity, and thought, 'That's not really where I see myself, making art for rich elitist people.'

"I see art as a tool for the proletariat. I was into skateboarding and punk rockers and getting into Beastie Boys, Run DMC, Public Enemy, N.W.A, Boogie Down Productions, Slick Rick, Ice-T. The hip-hop stuff had the same spirit of DIY—build new songs off of preexisting raw material. The same spirit in a different aesthetic. Rooting for the underdog. That was what I was doing. I considered myself the underdog and I wanted to bond with people who considered themselves outsiders."

One doesn't get too far along the misfit journey before realizing that so many traditional tools, maps, and cheat codes prove to be useless for our needs. We have been systematically handed manufactured answers without being told that they only fit very limited, established problems.

The unstructured nature of the misfit world demands an active engagement that is both frightening and exciting. Luckily, these factors play off each other to inspire impromptu creative problem-solving. This cannot be taught, because it's not a lesson to be studied and learned—it's motivation. And motivation must be activated from within, engaging you in the moment so that you may not even be aware of what you are doing until after a solution, a new tool for the task, has been discovered.

School and institutional systems pretend to deliver us to the same destination—the answer—by a very different means. They teach us to sit down passively and wait to be told the proper ways of the world. We are taught that this is how one learns. But in order to take that first step away from conventionality into the misfit unknown, you tap into an energy that explores unorthodox solutions.

In junior high, Tony's misfit obsession ran so hot that he went to his failing run-down skatepark every day. But there was a problem. Nobody else in his school skated. It was too far to bike and he wasn't old enough for his driver's license. Oh well, that's life, right? You tried. Easier to play football on the field that is part of the school. Join an official club with a school-designated meeting area. Maybe sign up for a group activity where parents join forces to carpool their kids.

Aware that no prebaked solution awaited him, Tony wasn't prepared to *not* skateboard after school every day. The school district's border ended near the town where the skatepark was located, so he figured out all the different routes that the school buses drove to deliver kids home. He began getting on the "wrong" bus to arrive closest to his "right" des-

tination, where he'd skate to his outcast clubhouse to sweat, laugh, earn scabs, and learn tricks until his dad picked him up later in the evening.

"Right from the beginning people believe what they are told," Marilyn vos Savant said in an interview, "and they never learn to think independently." Who is vos Savant? Only one of the smartest people in the world. Like, literally. Like, the highest IQ ever scored in Guinness World Records. And what does absolutely crushing the most traditional intelligence metric get her—a one-way ticket to Misfitville. She's so smart that it allowed her to see how the system that graded her, elevated her, is not at all what makes you "smart."

"I think one of the problems is compulsory schooling," she said in an interview. "The child is taught, right from the beginning, that it is a passive process. They simply try to believe everything they are told."

So what does she think makes the difference? "I think motivation plays a much greater part than people realize," she said. Except motivation is a tricky thing to recognize in ourselves. Aim it in the "wrong" direction and you will not be told that you are blessed with an admirable attribute, you'll be labeled stubborn, problematic, inflexible. You will be declared disruptive, a bad influence, misguided, accused of not using your motivation "properly."

I lacked a deep comprehension of this issue until recently, when my son casually asked if I knew about "functional fixedness"—FF. I'd never heard the term before, but who doesn't like alliterations? Cooper thought the concept was pretty funny, considering how he had been raised. He explained that it was like needing to hit a nail in and being unable to complete the task without a hammer, the tool specifically designated for that task.

What was this nonsense he was talking about?

Was it possible that people were intentionally that self-restrictive?

"Unable to complete a task" because there isn't a specifically labeled

tool for the job? Immediately, I thought about C.R. Stecyk III creating his first skateboard.

"Nothing existed, so we improvised," Stecyk said. "We scavenged to make skateboards. I'd search for shelves in the trash or maybe pull fence boards out and go behind the roller rink looking for discarded roller skates. I'd go down to the yacht basin and look in the trash cans for Converse Sea Stars. The boat guys would get fish guts on their shoes and toss them. They'd smell like shit because they had fish slime on them, but they were free. We were hitting nails in with pieces of concrete from the boatyard and skating off. It was feral like that. I was golden."

Absolutely zero of Stecyk's story followed functional fixedness, and no designated tools were involved. The dude is so opposite that he might as well be allergic to the FF notion—no stopping the process by waiting for a hammer, hand me that chunk of broken concrete. Was it really possible that people were so fixed in their thinking that they wouldn't have been capable of spontaneously adapting and performing a single one of Stecyk's actions?

Unable to process the extent of this creative blockage, I looked FF up and found this: "Functional fixedness is the inability to realize that something known to have a particular use may also be used to perform other functions. When one is faced with a new problem, functional fixedness blocks one's ability to use old tools in novel ways."

Ahh . . . got it. Some compassion flowered inside of me. Functional fixedness is a disability that afflicts passionate conformists. As a misfit in a "normal" group setting like work, school, or communal activities, you may have already experienced crashing into FF head-on when problems have presented themselves. A solution may have popped into your head and you may have voiced it, only to see it voted down by committee or dismissed by some form of conventional authority. The reasoning? Improper. It's wrong according to an invisible rule, located smack in the

middle of our misfit blind spot. Without knowing how, you have broken the "it's not done that way" law.

"But *why* is it not done that way?"

Stop asking stupid questions.

Get back in the box.

"Because *nobody* does it that way."

Stop using chunks of concrete to problem-solve.

And by the way—your shoes smell like dead fish.

Look at misfit subcultures and you'll see the explosively creative manner in which outcasts jailbreak objects locked into a functional fixedness. Card games become wildly imaginative, complex fantasy worlds. Dice go from gambling tools to complex formulas determining power shifts that decide life-or-death outcomes when battling cannibal elves in cursed swamps. Aerosol radiator paint becomes a portable communication tool conveying messages with stylized words and images on walls. Songs and beats are scratched, chopped up, repeated, elongated, stuttered, and taped back together to create entirely new types of music. Goodwill clothes are cut and resewn, zippers added, spray-paint stencils applied to make new fashions. Roller skates are broken apart and nailed onto miniature surfboards. Traditional haircuts are deconstructed, styles turned upside down and sideways while food dye or Kool-Aid packets bring colors not found in nature to the tops of heads.

MARK MOTHERSBAUGH As kids, we were always rough with our albums, and somebody had scratched my sister's Bee Gees album. That record was on the turntable and I put the needle down and it got to a certain part of the song, hit the scratch, and kept skipping back and skipping back. It kept doing it over and over again, and

> I went and got a guitar and started playing along with it. This was before I even imagined what electronic versions of that would be like—this was a start in the direction where I was looking for sounds and ideas in music that hadn't been explored yet. As far as my sister was concerned, the record was ruined. My problem was that I didn't have the technology to play along and record it so I could write a song to it—I just jammed with the Bee Gees in an arrhythmic repetitive loop.

The traditionalist reaction to this anti–functional fixedness behavior? Almost always there will be a version of "it's not done that way" referencing back to traditional rules of operation, as if that were all the proof needed to stop thinking.

Dr. Jon Freeman experienced the widespread incomprehension that greeted Dungeons & Dragons in the 1970s. "What D&D did was change the construct in the same way that certain music genres change constructs about how people listen to music."

He remembers trying to explain to his parents the motivation behind the strange noises coming from the area where he and his friends were engaging in a campaign. Shouts about checking the players' handbook to see that a fireball has a twenty-foot radius, not diameter, and if it still burned them. "If I told my parents I was playing a game of Strat-O-Matic baseball and was trying to explain how it was a simulation, they'd ask if it had a bat or a ball? No, it uses dice and strategy [within the rules of baseball] so it's just a game—a very easy concept for them to understand. If I tell them I'm playing a game where there are swords and we're fighting monsters . . . and there's no board?" Not so easy for people to understand if they're locked into an inflexible idea of what a board game is.

"D&D changed the idea of what a game can be," Dr. Jon says. "Just like in music, just like in art, just like in anything creative, when somebody breaks the mold, creates something new, a lot of people have very strong and negative reactions to it because they don't understand what it is."

Similar to how Dr. Jon and his D&D campaigns reimagined the traditional board game, young Roger slowly recognized how artists were reconceptualizing the walls all around his regular walks through the city. If museums and galleries gatekeep an antiquated, entitled opinion of what "real" art is, refusing to recognize innovative expressions from kids refusing to obey what art school teaches, well, some anti–functional fixedness is in order. The OG aerosol artists creating a new style responsible for works that now sell for tens of millions looked at the well-lit interior gallery walls and problem-solved that they could use the other side of the wall to showcase their art.

Stecyk said as much to me years ago, but it felt like he used a chunk of mental concrete to deliver the message, breaking some fixed way of thinking that I had unknowingly let set. **"The only difference between the Sistine Chapel ceiling and the graffiti on a sewer wall is marketing."**

STACY PERALTA "As a teenager, my friend and I had a debate with his father. His father wasn't condemning surfing, but he was saying, 'I don't see the point in what you guys do. I don't see an objective. You guys spend so much time devoted to this thing—so much time! You leave at dark in the morning, you drive the coast and find a wave, you spend hours out there, and when you step back on the beach, everything that you have done has vanished. You have nothing to show for it—there's no objective.'

"I said, 'What's the objective of basketball?' He said, 'There's a clear objective. There are two teams and they face off against each other to see which team can get the most balls in the basket, and whoever wins in the allotted amount of time wins. And they go on to beat the next team until there is a champion. That is the objective.'

"I wasn't able to articulate an answer back then, but now I would say that every time I got on my board and skimmed across a wave I felt beautiful. And every kid needs to find something in their life they feel beautiful doing. When you feel beautiful doing something, you feel strong, you feel connected to yourself, you feel con-nected to the world, and you feel connected to people around you. When I did it, that's how I felt. When I skateboarded, that's how I felt. When I watched my friends do it, that's how I felt—they were beautiful. That's why we did it, because it plugged us into who we were. Everybody needs that. Everybody is searching for that in their lives. We just happened to do it at a time with an activity that was frowned upon by society at large because they didn't understand it because there was no structure to it and there was nobody making any money off it.

"As soon as they finally put structure to surfing and as soon as people could make money off of surfing, people understood it, because they can understand competition and they can understand money. That doesn't mean they understand surfing. The money and the competition were a medium upon which society could look at surfing now and see it for something else."

12

The Joy of Obstacles

"Obstacle" is a word that pops up a lot in skateboard talk, and from what I can discern, the self-help community really likes throwing it around too. Oxford defines an obstacle as "a thing that blocks one's way or prevents or hinders progress." Now, if this book was written for people who like self-help books, perhaps I'd patent a cute name for a process that teaches you to bulldoze life obstacles with some newfound mind powers. But I don't know how to do that, because my misfit passion has taught me to deeply appreciate all the hard, impassable aspects of obstacles—it's not their nature or placement that we want to change. Our misfit passions directly challenge us to step back to view them anew with an open creativity.

The essence of skateboarding comes from looking at and finding joy within the struggle to ride something *not* specifically designed for that purpose. Imagine participating in the Super Bowl only to find that you're playing on a circular football field, or competing for the Stanley Cup on convex ice. Skateboarders thrive and find identity in that sort of spontaneous adaptation.

"You don't see the world the same way others do, because you're looking for embankments and ledges and things to ride," Tony says. "You have completely shifted your outlook."

Empty pools were considered useless eyesores during the California drought of the 1970s or, even worse, hazards for people and pets to fall into, but skaters reimagined them as roller coaster rides allowing for accelerating pumps through corners. Handrails designed for stability became dangerous playground slides to skim down. Twenty-foot-tall desert pipes intended for massive water movement transformed into zero-gravity chambers when ridden up beyond vertical. Curbs, designed to "curb" movement and direct the flow of sewage and traffic, became fun obstacles to grind and slide on, even pop over with a trick called the "no-comply" because the skater isn't complying with the intended action. "Two hundred years of American technology has unwittingly created a massive cement playground of unlimited potential," Stecyk infamously wrote, "but it was the minds of eleven-year-olds that could see that potential."

"There is an apocalyptic nature to skateboarding that is really intriguing," Stacy says. "No matter how many obstacles the terrain finds, it is going to make it more interesting to skate. All the odds that go against skateboarding somehow make it more interesting and more appealing. That offers a lot in identity and self-expression."

Skaters use obstacles as a way to discover their personal potential, and all misfits can do the same. There is a joy and pride created when skaters reimagine something and envision how to ride it and then push our physical abilities—reflexes, timing, board control—to a point where we can IRL what we imagined in our minds. As a culture, we are *very* serious about this concept. There are even "rules" about how much you can modify an existing obstacle before it stops delivering the same culture cred that comes from adapting to a hostile environment. And as misfits, we all have to deal with hostile environments.

Ever walked on a sidewalk that has erupted, a tree root pushing up a

section of concrete at an angle? Skaters will drive a hundred miles to skate one messed up in just the right way next to a bus stop that they can tailslide or front-boardslide on. Could they build a wooden ramp and place it down the block next to the closest bus stop in less time than it takes to drive there? For sure, but that would not be an obstacle and the accomplishment would be worth considerably less in misfit currency.

Mark would deconstruct electric guitars with his brother, a wiz at "circuit bending," and rewire inputs, solder new contacts, and make the assembly-line product sound "broken" in just the right way. They'd experiment until Mark would warp it enough so that it played a sound unlike any other guitar, projecting a full postapocalyptic bomb-blast vibe with distortion pedals duct-taped to the body, wires exploding out, cords plugging into new inputs. (Check out the live *SNL* version of "Satisfaction" by DEVO to see the Mad Max guitar.)

Of course, obstacles come in all shapes and sizes—physical, mental, and metaphorical and all in your face. But, hey, there is a reason that you turned away from conformity and its assurances of patted heads and predictable outcomes. This is the type of motivated education you crave, and even though it's scary and stressful, it becomes thrilling when accompanied by the awareness that it can unlock hidden aspects of yourself.

Status quo society will try to protect itself by throwing obstacles all over alternative routes to curb the masses from accidentally operating differently. Can't do that job unless you have a bachelor's degree. Can't be considered attractive with that skin or a nose or eyes shaped like that. That's not how real artists express themselves. That's not a real sport. To a misfit, dealing with obstacles does not reflect the disobedience that the traditionalists see ("No Skateboarding" signs are now just a part of urban scenery), but rather motivation to find an original way to problem-solve.

Michelle employed this approach to an obstacle that was, literally, skateboarding. Not at all interested in my specific misfit passion, she reimagined aspects of it into something she could "ride." In the early 2000s, Michelle showed up by herself at a skateboard park with her roller skates. Now, in the early 1980s a few roller skaters briefly rode alongside skateboarders at skateparks, but the quad-wheel fad had disappeared by then. For decades roller-skating was totally absent from skateboard parks.

Michelle was well aware of how Rollerbladers and skateboarders had a long-standing Jets-versus-Sharks beef, and while it may have mellowed, she was not sure how welcomed she'd be in skateboard territory. Were roller skates close enough to Rollerblades to guarantee the same blowback? To make matters worse, she picked a raw DIY park in Philadelphia "illegally" built by skaters, making it an even more territorial situation.

Self-conscious, scared, she forced herself to walk into an area intention-ally filled with obstacles and sat down to lace up her skates.

A nearby skater saw her lacing up. "Are you seriously going to do that?"

Now, coming from a stranger, that is one loaded phrase that can be taken in a variety of ways. Michelle replied in the affirmative, preparing herself for abuse. "That is so fucking cool!" the skateboarder said. "Those are baby skateboards. You're really going to do that here? *Can* you do that?"

Indeed she could. Michelle was experimenting, finding a new way to ride her roller skates, on her way to ushering in a new scene that reflected her aggressive and inclusive approach. Eventually, she'd make her own powerfully innovative video with a skateboard filmer, a first of its kind where she was seeing and utilizing urban terrain as a playground like Stecyk had said about skateboarders.

Nobody expected the video to do anything, because there had never been anything like it, but it blew up around the world with millions of views, igniting the street roller-skating scene. Michelle is so strong-willed that she didn't drop her passion in order to do something preexisting, instead she took how they did it and circuit-bent it all to hell to make her own music. "It opened up a world for me," she says. The scene she helped build around this new type of roller-skating attracted a totally different demographic than skateboarding did.

Tony likewise had some serious obstacles that he needed to figure out. He was so short and skinny, so "weak," that when he started skate-boarding he had to battle the laws of physics on top of learning how to progress on a skateboard. Beyond a featherweight, he literally could not generate enough momentum to propel himself out of the bowls and into the air.

The accepted, dare we say "normal" way of doing aerials at the time was more muscular: Riders had to grab their board as they rode up the transition and use the momentum to yank themselves into the air. No matter how hard Tony pumped to gain momentum, he found himself barely able to pop air. He was going so slow that bending down essentially pumped the brakes on the pendulum swing.

But Tony didn't look at his heroes and assume their way was the only way to do airs—he looked at his heroes and saw how they innovated and invented new tricks. No other skater that Tony knew of had solved his particular problem, so he began using his obstacle to learn a new technique. What if he waited and didn't bend down to grab his board until he was already weightless in the air? "It was more functional to how I moved and how I could do it," Tony says. "It was more desperate—the way I made it work for me. **I couldn't do it the way that other people did it, and these people were more experienced or more celebrated so I didn't have a choice but to figure it out on my own.**"

Entirely unintentionally, Tony developed a technique that allowed for more technical tricks and ushered in a new era of progressive skating. Today, what was once called "late grab" style is the way every skateboarder does airs.

Misfit cultures evolve with enough elasticity to allow for progressive changes like these. "I certainly couldn't create a new way of playing ball sports," Tony says, "so when I started doing my own thing in skateboarding I didn't think I was creating a movement. The techniques I created were out of desperation, but they became the standard because people realized that they were a more efficient and functional way of doing it, and that was due to my limitations."

13

A PhD in Fence Climbing

The cool part of getting this far in the misfit journey is that you start to be inspired by how other nonconformists learn. Misfitting forces you to operate outside prescribed pathways and develop a new technique, because there is no other choice when you're beyond the fringe—there are no maps to follow when you're traveling in unmapped territory.

Often forced to reject a traditional educational template that can be aggressively unsupportive (not to mention expensive), misfits develop their own system of learning, allowing them to stay true to their culture. How did Ed go from having a friend sit him down and explain how a camera's shutter and exposure worked to his winning awards, having international exhibits, and being paid by some of the world's biggest fashion brands to shoot catalogs? How did he go from jr. ninja dazzled over a skater ollieing up a curb to winning professional skateboarding contests as a teenager with no coach, no training facility, and no program a few years later?

"There was definitely no coach," Ed says. "A major way skaters learn is through video—a new one would come out with some new shit in it and you'd think, *Holy crap,* that's possible? The next day you're trying those tricks, and that pushes the boundaries for you."

Misfits learn to inspire and educate each other, feeding into a perpetual loop of boundary-breaking progression. "It was the same with meeting up with a bunch of skaters from other areas," Ed says. "It felt like a learning incubator, with kids from other cities coming and introducing a weird trick and then you'd adopt it, absorb it into your style. You learn through osmosis."

The love of a misfit passion provides the motivation to extract needed data from whatever source is available in order to progress. The desire to level up and release more enjoyment turns us into data-mining beasts. My mom told me much later that she was left flabbergasted after overhearing teenage me talk to a store employee about my misfit passion—she had no idea how, when, or where I had gained so much knowledge about my esoteric interest, because I had done it on my own. The process had been hidden because it was so outside conventional templates, but if outcasts want to progress, they naturally adapt.

Learning to reimagine and ride obstacles is a necessary misfit skill, but there are also draconian restrictions demanding a different approach. Controlling progression is a favored conformist technique for retaining control. If there is one thing they really get off on, it's erecting fences to regulate social movement, often via education. Conformists can exert control by discrediting achievements as missing official accreditation and negating accomplishments as being out-of-bounds and therefore worthless. Don't have a college alma mater to define you? You really trying to get an introduction without a professor's recommendations? You need a degree—any degree, whether or not it's related—to even be considered for this job.

But misfits have already learned that lining up at the front door with everybody else, with their smart haircuts and resumes, isn't always the most effective way of pursuing goals. We are not asking for permission—we're pursuing a passion. **Out of necessity we've learned to climb fences**

and get in through back doors or rear windows. Some of us have done that literally, but every misfit learns to do those things metaphorically.

Our first step outside tradition wasn't authorized, so why would it change now? Misfits climb fences. Misfits trespass. Misfits learn how to elude and outrun guard dogs. Fences, after all, are what taught us that we misfit. Perhaps we held on to them and cried in protest like Tony, but our constant contact with them announces to us and everybody else that we have a problem.

The landscape they section off may be emotional, social, educational, familial, or occupational, but they are erected in the name of doing things the "right" way, the "proper" way. The people in charge of building, maintaining, and guarding said fences can only see us as trespassers, intentional rule breakers, but none of my outcast friends started with any intention of breaking rules—there were simply not a lot of available options.

Ed's paintings are sold in galleries and housed in museums all over the world, but he never attended art college or studied under a master painter. He acted on his artistic interest and used the graphic nature of the skateboard industry as an unconventional opportunity to get a foothold on the fence around the established art gallery scene.

"I was always interested in art as a kid, but I don't know when the point where I would consider myself an artist happened," Ed says, tracing how he entered the often fenced-in art world. "I was probably kinda late, because I turned pro as a skateboarder at eighteen. I was really conflicted about my art, because I didn't consider myself good. I didn't know what I was doing, but I had made that vow to myself that I was going to draw my own graphics for my pro model skateboard."

Ed came up with an image of a cat to screen on the bottom skateboard, and operating in a state of high motivation and equally heightened uncertainty, maybe even fear, he pushed himself into an unauthorized area. "It had a folksy feel to it, a Howard Finster type of feel. I was super stressed out. I was super scared about putting it out there, so self-conscious that in my first magazine ad for the board, I wrote: 'BUY ED TEMPLE-TON'S BOARD, IT'S THE ONE WITH THE CRAPPY GRAPH-ICS.' I was comparing it to more polished skateboard graphics, and it was a case of these clearly not being the same thing at all—mine was actual shit, but I wanted to do it myself."

Ed just crushed it at explaining the universally messy emotions that come with operating outside of functional fixedness, where assurances of "doing it right" are vanquished but at the same time an uncontrollable urge won't stop pushing you into the unknown. Ed's unconventional experiences with misfit education via skateboarding provided confidence to proceed without the official designation of his work being any "good."

"Even though I was super stressed out that it wasn't going to be good, I thought that some kids who saw it hanging in the shops would feel the same thing that I did when I saw a Chris Miller board with graphics that he had created on it," Ed says. "I was hoping they'd see my board and think, Oh, Ed did that himself! And even though it's shitty, it connects to us. Through the years I've heard from people that they liked it because the graphic was so different and not all polished and rad-looking."

Ed didn't conform to court head pats and art award ribbons. His passion to express punched through any preconceived values—even his own—of what constitutes "real" art. One misfit passion showed him how to connect to another and to another and then another like footholds in a chain-link fence. But looking back on Ed's recollection, he shows us the secret to climbing fences—concentrate on the motivation rather than the fence.

Trust me on this—you are not going to be climbing any fences if you're not motivated. You have to get past being told that it's forbidden, that you can snag and rip clothes, that you can fall off from great heights.

But once you realize that you can climb a fence, that there are rebellious ways to arrive at supposedly restricted areas of life that open up other opportunities—that is a potent source of power.

I'd argue that honing a willingness to climb fences is one way to refine an approach that keeps your style, your uniqueness, in your expression. This doesn't mean you can't benefit from traditional education (the last thing we want to do is make a list of rules restricting ourselves), but the master misfits I know intuitively find alternative ways to use their lessons learned, regardless of how they gathered the information.

"Learn to master your craft and then learn how to fuck it up," Seneca

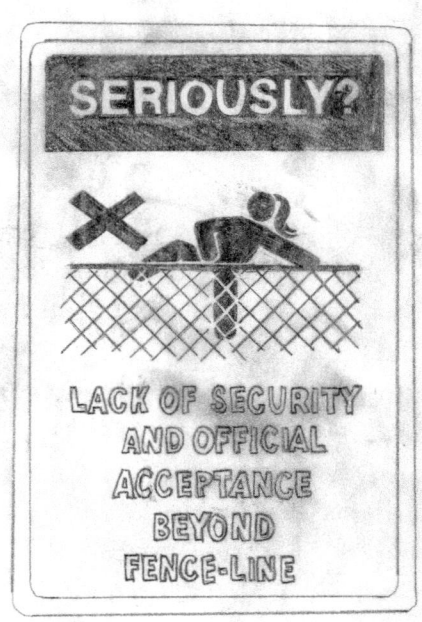

says. "It's a cruder way of saying 'Learn what the rules are, break them, and then make them your own.'"

Shepard went to the prestigious Rhode Island School of Design, only to hijack the prescribed lesson plan. "The summer after my freshman year, I applied for a position at a screen-printing studio," he says. There was only one problem: "I didn't know how to do photo emulsions yet and I had said that I did know so I went [to the screen printing studio] and gave a dude a twelve-pack and he said he'd teach me everything. I was working at a skate shop, printing T-shirts for them and going to school. I was nineteen, having responsibilities, making things that determine the aesthetics at the age when people are telling you that you don't know anything and you're too young, stand in line and wait your turn—I thought, *I'm just bypassing all that.*"

Make no mistake—when you climb fences and use chunks of concrete instead of the hammer, there will be aggressive pushback at some point. "It can put people out of their comfort zone because this isn't the way it normally is, but is that a bad thing?" Shepard says of his approach to learning as well as communicating via street art. "I looked at it like some people might appreciate that and other people will be irritated by it, but at least I'm not just accepting things for the way they are. Heidegger's theory of phenomenology says people become numb to their surroundings and they need unexpected experiences to reawaken a sense of wonder and to make them analyze things in a way that is more rigorous."

Mark avoided the military draft by earning a scholarship to Kent State, and while he was no longer bullied for being different, he wasn't exactly respecting the school's fences. While loving the access to tools and knowledge, he immediately broke from the expected structure.

"I jettisoned the curriculum that was assigned to me to get a bachelor's degree," Mark says. "I thought, *You know what? I don't even care*

about a bachelor's degree. There are things that I want to learn, and what I want to learn is how to make real art."

Future bandmate Jerry, a year ahead, told Mark about an advanced conceptual art class that he'd like. Mark lacked the prerequisites to get in, but we know how fenced-off areas can encourage fence climbing. "This is the first year they're using computers for class registration," Jerry said. "You could fill in anything you want and they'll believe you." Mark faked whatever was deemed necessary, input the wrong data into the university's machinery, and started taking classes he technically wasn't allowed to.

This approach makes perfect sense coming from a guy who would sing "Monkey men all in business suits / Teachers and critics / All dance the poot" to millions of misfits around the world. "I started forgetting all about the curriculum needed to get a diploma," Mark says. "I wasn't going to be an art teacher. I cherry-picked all the classes I was interested in and stopped prepping for graduation. I never graduated, but later on I did get an honorary doctorate in Humane Letters."

"I wasn't going to art school to get a degree," Seneca says, agreeing with Mark, "I was going to learn."

Marilyn vos Savant, that lady with one of the highest IQs, said, "I think the most exciting thing is the dawn of understanding." That excitement she's describing sounds a lot like what it feels like when the soles of your feet hit the dirt on the other side of a successful fence climb.

"We are not here to do what has already been done," the art teacher Robert Henri said over a hundred years ago in his famous book *The Art Spirit*. The simplicity of the sentence makes the sentiment appear ludicrously obvious, but if you're remembering it as motivation whenever you see part of your life fenced off for conformist reasons, it becomes a compelling mantra to live by.

MICHELLE "If there are problems to solve, then you are in thriving mode. There are already embedded ways of doing things, and it can make people feel that they have to have all this stuff before they start to solve any problems. When it is not all copacetic and there is some resistance and there is dysfunction, then you are in a problem-solving mode with other people, which connects you. I totally resonate with that. You have to be able to embrace the mess. You have to embrace that you do not fit in and that there is work to be done and it's messy because it doesn't exist—the results you want do not exist. You have to lean into the discomfort and deal with the mess, and you're going to expose all the messy parts of you as you do that."

14

I've Fallen and I Can't Stop Learning

A misfit life is one chock-full of falls, of fails, of crashes. Emotionally and socially, you will find yourself unexpectedly on your ass, tumbling out of control, maybe lurching to a stop knocked out. That's why skateboarding is an easy metaphor for this book—it takes so many aspects of our journey and puts them into slapstick physicality. Rejection from public spaces. Devalued activity. Harassed by authority. Innovative DIY approaches and subsequent crashes. The misfit life forces you to consistently deal with something most people spend their lives avoiding—crashing—and we do that by fashioning a different cost-accounting that allows us to extract data as we ride the fail afresh.

Slipping on a banana peel has got to be one of the oldest sight gags in human history, and skaters do it on repeat when skateboarding. Like Eskimos and their multitude of names for types of snow, we have a long list of ways to fail. The "Credit Card" is when the board shoots up and swipes between your legs. The "Scorpion" is landing on your chest and your legs curling up behind your head. A "Magic Carpet Ride" is when you jump off your board and accidentally land back on it out of control. "Wheel Bite" is when your wheels rub against the deck violently, pulling the e-brake demonstrating Newton's Law of Motion about objects in motion unfortunately staying in motion.

Lots of cute names and black humor, but they show how intimately aligned skateboarders are with unmitigated failure. When we lose, we can't blame the refs, point an accusing finger at a teammate, locate the excuse as to why we'd normally have won. Instead, skaters put slams and crashes in our videos with bowling-pins-being-knocked-over sounds, we laugh when we and our friends do it—unless they cross the line into serious injury—and we expect to be in the middle of our own catastrophic fails, out of control and twisting to maneuver into the least damaging position before the point of impact.

When skateboarders fail, it is obscenely obvious and such an integral part of how we learn that there is no shame in consistently eating shit, of flunking the test, getting it all wrong, not being up to the task, bombing it. Stripping emotions out of something most of humankind considers embarrassing gifts you an objectivity that allows for an incredibly intense method of learning. Misfits willingly study at the school of failure. The Big F solidifies an engaged misfit's sense of self-confidence, because what had appeared as a door slammed shut changes into a threshold to be crossed when you crash through it enough times.

To get to this point, though, you have to do some serious deprogramming, because all around us in traditional society shame and embarrassment are interwoven into failure. This, naturally, encourages people to follow protocol, sign up for the risk-averse life of conformity. Misfits, on the other hand, know that we are exploring unknown areas and that the only way to extract knowledge is through exploration, which is naturally full of unexpected results. **The unexpected is undertaken with excitement over the precious information hidden within the experience.** Misfits understand that learning how to fall is not simply a way to avoid injury, it's a modus operandi for how to continue exploring.

STACY PERALTA "When we developed pool skating, the most important technique we developed was how to fall. If you couldn't learn how to fall then you couldn't ride a pool. Falling is failing. Failing is one of the most important things you can learn in your life. Absolutely one of the key reasons I have been successful in my life is because I understand how to fail. I understand the ramifications in failing and how it sets off so many bad qualities in me, and because I know what it does to me, I know how to circumvent it. Yeah, people say you have to persevere, but you have to fail and you have to understand what happens to you when you fail. Self-pity. Self-destruction. Giving up. Giving in. Depression. Victimhood. It can really derail some people. If I can circumvent those traits, then I'm learning to fail. If I want to keep learning new stuff, then part of learning something new is knowing I am going to fail again."

By objectively observing ourselves fail, misfits open themselves up to spontaneous education, building a relationship with chaos in order to pull data from it to problem-solve and learn new things about ourselves.

There is pressure to being a misfit, a background hum of danger that wavers in volume, but it's part of the beautiful buildup when you begin learning how to progress through the chaos of failure. Maybe that chaos manifests physically like in skateboarding or maybe it's emotional, familial, psychological, or social disorder. What directs us through failure and danger is the passion for our misfit activities. The danger of failure, which seems to be front and center for conventional people, gets pushed back when our misfit passion ignites and we move closer to our unconventional goal.

I spent days on my driveway trying to kickflip my board hundreds, thousands of times over and over until I made it. I never once stopped to think about what a loser I appeared to be, how I might break my ankle or wrist. To my neighbors, I must have looked and sounded like a record unable to get beyond a scratch, skipping failure on an endless loop projecting my lack of talent, but to me every single mistake transmitted clues until I learned where to position my feet, what pressure to apply to my tail to pop the board into the air, the timing to kick my front foot out to initiate the rotation, the recoil of that foot to get it back up in order to land atop the board after the flip. And then pray that I didn't whip out when I landed leaning too far back.

Every single failure produced a teeny Lego piece to help me stack one on another until I had enough to build my accomplishment. And Lego pieces, as anybody who has stepped on a stray one knows, can be either painful or snapped together to become joyful acts of imagination.

I didn't know what I was doing—there was no design on how to go about learning skateboarding, as Ed said earlier. Desire led the way. Embracing any misfit passion imparts this approach intuitively. "It's easy for me to tell you this now, but I'm not going to tell you that I knew it then," Sacha says. "But I've never been afraid to fail, because I wasn't formally taught. I didn't really know what was proper or correct and I didn't know what would be a failure, so I would try and I would, of course, fail. It's easy for me to say this now, but I think failure is the best teacher you can have. If you can fail a couple of times, you're going to be able to improve, if you keep with it. Most people fail and they give up: 'I'm a failure.' Failure is the best learning tool. I don't think most people understand that at a young age, and I understand that, but I was

never afraid to fail, because no one told me if what I was doing was right or wrong."

> **SHEPARD FAIREY** "Conceptualizing in a vacuum only goes so far—you have to start doing. Experimenting leads to breakthroughs, because when you experiment what you thought was going to be the solution ends up not being the solution, but you discover something else and there is a chain reaction of evolution that comes out of that. It's overcoming the fear of failure, because when you start doing, you're going to fail. Failure is totally a way to learn."

Let's take an extreme example of the importance of failure, and have the misfit involved walk us through it. Tony has been inventing tricks since he was thirteen years old. This requires him to first envision it and then start the long process of experimenting in an unknown void to figure out how to manifest it into real life. The first phase is just throwing himself and his board out there in the closest approximation that he can guess to see how everything reacts together. From this he gets a baseline with the variables—how much speed he needs, angle of approach, timing when to shift body weight, does he need to wind up or rearrange foot placement, etc.

This is the same for every skateboarder, regardless of skill level, and I've seen both pros learning McTwists and newbies learning basic axle stalls get SO excited about extracting a lynchpin revelation from a failure that brings them closer to the solve. Tony did this famously in front of the biggest audience that skateboarding has ever seen when he failed on repeat while learning how to land the 900 on live television during the Best Trick Contest at the 1999 X Games.

"With the 900 I didn't have foam pits, instructions—all I had was trial and error," Tony says. For over a decade, he had failed hundreds of times in his attempt to land it, but he'd been extracting knowledge from each experience. "I knew I had all the pieces of the puzzle and at some point I knew I could fit them all together, but there were so many false starts along the way and moments that were very discouraging and painful. I learned from hard slams that even if the takeoff is wrong, even if I miss grabbing my board, I need to continue with my spin. That saved me many times."

The 900 was such an unknown experience and the fails exacted such a brutal punishment that Tony wasn't able to continuously attempt it like he would other tricks. He had to fine-tune how to fail. "It wasn't something that was passed down to me, and it seems counterintuitive, but I gave up my spin on an early attempt and landed on my back and smacked harder than I had before. Secondly, I learned there is a minimum of speed I need and I cannot force a faster spin, like I can with other tricks. I did that once and hit the wall of the ramp before I was prepared to."

So now failure had a new barrier—a limit on how many attempts were possible before he was physically unable to continue. Year after year, Tony kept track of what he was learning from his ongoing failure. "Those were bullet points," he says, "a baseline of how it could possibly work." After years of staccato attempts and recovery, he snapped some of the pieces together. "If I had all the elements, if I had the right speed and takeoff then those were the times I would really try to make it. I'd only get a good attempt every fourth or fifth try. I couldn't waste them, because it was so exhausting and took so much effort to get to that point."

And when he was confident that he had unlocked the mystery of the

trick, right at that point failure would continually reveal how far away he actually was. We were alone in a dusty San Diego warehouse and I filmed Tony as he bailed a few 900 attempts before popping up excitedly, nodding to himself, so hyped that he seemed to be skipping up the stairs to the top of the ramp, endorphins illuminating new calculus formulas in his head that would finally reveal one of skateboarding's most sought-after tricks.

"At one point I thought I had all the pieces and could put it together," Tony says of that day. He dropped in, boosting an air to get speed and then blasting into the air six feet above the roughly twelve-foot-high ramp into a tight spin before winding himself into another spin as he began to descend, two full rotations completed above the ramp. He put the wheels down in what appeared to be a clean landing but found himself unable to not lean forward and stop spinning. He rode for a moment and then pile-drove himself, at speed, into the ramp.

"I broke my rib," Tony says. "I thought I had the proper technique and commitment and everything it took to make it happen. When I fully committed to it with my skill set that I had developed for decades, it didn't work and I got hurt. I gave it everything I had and came up with an injury that wasn't debilitating, but it was shocking. That was wildly discouraging, to the point that I thought, *I have to put this on the shelf or maybe forget about it forever.* I don't think I ever closed it off and thought: *This cannot be done.* But it was such a setback that I thought, *Maybe I don't have what it takes.*"

Even when a misfit is trained in retooling failure into something helpful, there will be moments when that resolve, that "riding the obstacle," is put to the test.

"I'd never pursued a trick for so long and not succeeded at it," Tony says. "Then, at the 1999 X Games, I had some extra time after making my trick and the other elements were in place. There was a really solid ramp, which was rare in that day. I had the support of the crowd and my peers behind me. It helped me put myself at a risk that no other scenario was going to. I was prepared to take a huge slam."

It's fitting that, in true misfit fashion, the most famous mainstream skateboarding accomplishment wasn't even planned. "The first attempt was almost more for show—here's what I'd like to do next in my best-trick succession," Tony says. "This is what it looks like! But then with every attempt, I had the right amount of speed, the right takeoff. I took advantage of that opportunity. I did the same mistake where I leaned too far forward, but because I didn't get hurt when I landed, that was the key. So how do you remedy that? Well, you lean back upon landing, shift your weight. So the next one I tried I shifted my weight, but it was too far and I fell backward. That was it—split the difference and make it work. There was a little bit of luck in that I didn't repeat my same mistake and break my rib again."

Not only did Tony exhibit primo misfit perseverance, but how his peers, technically his *competitors,* reacted showcased the misfit culture behind their passion. Tony actually landed the 900 after the officially allotted time for the contest, but none of his fellow competitors protested—they had all stopped skateboarding and gathered around giving him support, feeling a communal joy in barrier-breaking.

The "official" clock had stopped and every skater—even the one who might have legitimately won the contest—ignored it. And when Tony finally rode away clean, everybody slid down the ramp, jumped the barriers to rush the ramp, and jumped on Tony, feeling that we had all won.

Tony did not develop a new misfit method of learning to land one of the most celebrated "alternative" tricks in history. He personally refined the misfit lesson on how to approach and systematically learn when entering unknown experiences to suit his extreme need. Hopefully, this is what will inspire readers of this book who don't skateboard to take the "I've fallen and I can't stop learning" lesson off a rolling toy and into life. Tony surely does.

"It affects my approach to life—parenting, making important decisions, finances," Tony says. "I have plenty of missteps, and I embrace them. I have learned through skating not to repeat that same mistake, and that can be a breakthrough in your way of living. If you keep making the same mistakes, then you're not learning anything. For some people that can become a comfort zone, and I don't want to live in a comfort zone. I don't want to live a life on repeat. I want to evolve."

When approaching your unconventional life with that mindset, expect to end up on your ass more than your conventional neighbor, but if your friends have similar derriere damage there will be a communal momentum. "When you see everyone else pushing themselves, you want to do it too," Ed says. "You think, *This hasn't been done before,* but your skill level is at a point where you can do things that haven't been done. There is a point of discovery that allows you to try something new. Then you realize that it isn't that hard, that this is within the skill set that you have. You use that to morph it into something else."

SEVEN

HYSTERICAL STRENGTH

15

Lift Thy Car

SHEPARD FAIREY: "It was a fascinating transition, because where I had not wanted to stand out for so many years, where I wanted to assimilate to every single trend for fear of being ridiculed for not being in step, all of a sudden, all the excitement was about being out of step with that stuff, going against that mentality. It's a shock when you realize that a lot of other people are desperate to be themselves and you have the courage to say, 'You guys have the whole conformity thing going on over here and I don't play by those rules.'"

At this point, you, my friend, are one strong mofo. It takes a lot of strength to get this far, except it probably doesn't register as any kind of power, might even feel like a desperate weakness.

When you're hanging off a cliff's edge by the fingertips, there is no pause to marvel at your strength.

"Every day now I get some sort of message that says my art or whatever I did meant so much to them." Ed pauses to make sure what he's about to say is in no way disrespectful to those he's impacted. "That's hard to handle, because a lot of it was just . . . I don't know how to describe it . . . 'survival'?"

When we feel we have no other choice, when it feels like survival, that can help you tap into amazing aspects of yourself to pull through. A mom lifting a car off her child. A lady fighting a full-sized polar bear with her bare hands. A guy ripping off a crushed car door to extract an injured driver. Moments like these are labeled "hysterical strength," which is when a perceived life-or-death situation activates feats of superhuman power.

Perhaps a secret of hysterical strength is that you lack objective awareness in the moment—there is *no choice* within your scope of vision. You are doing what you must to survive. Misfits, due to the very nature of their clashing nonconformity, are consistently pushed into critical situations, so it should come as no surprise that we've become accustomed to subconsciously forcing hysterical aspects of ourselves into action.

One direct result of this is how essential the do-it-yourself spirit has become to misfit culture. The DIY spirit isn't a specific skill set, it's an urge to manifest something necessary yet unavailable, something that lies beyond your expertise, and it's this hysterical strength that allows us to overwhelm raging self-doubt radiating from inexperience. It's misfit do-or-die, since nobody else is going to help.

"It wasn't strength," Stacy says about being forced to make the world's first action sports video. "It was, but a *weird* strength." It was "weird" in the sense that the person forcing Stacy into a critical situation was himself. "My strength is to sustain being vulnerable and weak and not let that

stop me. I was consumed with self-doubt, and the fact that I couldn't do what I was embarking to do but there was no choice, so I did it. There was no thought of, 'I have strength! I'm doing this!' No. It was more: 'I have no idea what I'm doing and I have no choice. I'm just going to do it.'"

This is a plus/minus of fringe culture—a lack of validation and existing frameworks initially starve confidence but eventually encourage spontaneous problem-solving requiring hysterical strength. Without being aware of the process, misfits DIY confidence and strength as they DIY solutions.

Compare this to conformist culture, which tends to sow doubt and emphasize weakness in order to halt impulsive forward momentum without official approval. "Leave it to the experts" is a common piece of dismissive advice, but what if you're creating something unconventional, something with no "experts"? What if your outcast status blocks immediate help? What if there are no existing examples of your specific project succeeding?

It's essential to understand that "successful" misfits are not necessarily any more determined than you. What allows them to consistently accomplish goals is how they react to overwhelming stress and anxiety. Stacy, for example, had no intention of directing his first film project, and if there had been a way to wriggle out, he admits he would have.

In 1983 there was no YouTube or internet, but VHS players had just been introduced to the general public. Stacy's friend had gone to film school, and pitched making a video for Stacy's skateboard brand. The idea of a home video showcasing fringe action sports was not even a concept, but Stacy knew this new medium would give the dynamic nature of this misfit passion another dimension. It was a good idea—let the friend who knows how to do it do it.

The day before the first day of shooting, he received a phone call from the director. "My friend was also a budding actor and he got a commercial and couldn't make the film anymore," Stacy says. The only problem being that Stacy had already rented the equipment. But being a seasoned misfit, a world champion in his passion, he was used to dealing with anxiety and stress and confidently took the reins, right?

"No!" Stacy says, recalling how anxiety played a failure loop in his head. "I had *no choice* but to do it myself! The chances of me screwing up were very large.

"It seemed to me that I wasn't going to be able to pull it off," he says.

With no idea how to operate the large rental cameras, clueless as to what various lenses did, he manically studied the included manual and showed up that first day extremely insecure . . . and that was when the will to survive that Ed talked about took over.

Stacy hoisted the massive camera onto his shoulder on the first day. He lined up the shot he imagined, pushed his head against the black rubber eyecup—the outside world blocked off except for what the lens would see and record—and hit the record button for the first time in his life.

"Once I saw the first footage of the first shoot, I thought, *Wow, this is really powerful,*" Stacy says, and that little glimmer of success forged a sense of responsibility. That little result didn't blow up his ego—instead it allowed Stacy to put more pressure on himself. *This has to happen,* Stacy thought. *People need to see this.*"

But then . . .

While shooting footage was one thing, it quickly became evident that editing it was a much more complex problem. Stacy looked at the raw footage that he'd somehow managed to capture and felt completely helpless, with no idea how to put it together.

"I was absolutely convinced that I could never be an editor," Stacy says.

"What happened was that I was looking for an editor to cut it and couldn't find anyone, but I had an editing machine at my place because I needed something that enabled me to look at the footage. I was looking at all the footage and one day I thought, *Let me just see if I can string together a run of Tony at the Del Mar skatepark.*"

"I did it and thought, *Huh, I did that, but if I can do it then it must be bad.* I kept doing it because I couldn't find an editor and I didn't know if it was any good, but I had no choice but to keep doing it and doing it."

Fingers aching and bleeding as you pull a door off. Fists balled up, a scream roaring out of you as you punch a polar bear. An entire car's movement measured in frantic fractions upward.

"Skateboarding taught me how to shoot and edit video, because I followed what I already understood about the rhythm of skateboarding and that got me out of my fear zone," Stacy says.

Since new, unexpected situations often feel overwhelming, finding ways to "get out of your fear zone" is vital. You'll notice that feats of hysterical strength are never possible if they're scheduled—anxiety, misfit flight-or-fight has to be activated. **The misfit lifestyle is about remaining open to unexpected critical situations because they stimulate incredible parts of yourself otherwise dormant.**

Stacy went from absolutely not wanting to be put in a certain situation to constantly putting himself into that position as he became an award-winning filmmaker.

"I understood skateboarding, and it was skateboarding that taught me how to be a filmmaker because I knew what I wanted it to look like," Stacy says. The traditional world decreed that you needed to be an actual filmmaker to make a film about alternative sports, but Stacy was the first to invert the formula so that you needed to be an actual skateboarder to make a skateboard film. There's no reason why you can't do the same in your own way with your passion.

Michelle never imagined herself leading a revolt to bring in a new type of alternative sport, but, like Stacy, she has a tendency to repeatedly push herself into critical situations. After leaving the structured world of college and then the less structured world of roller derby, she put herself on the hook for over a hundred grand in roller skate inventory with an unproven store that she was running with no previous experience. Michelle didn't crater when sales weren't popping, instead, she activated her hysterical strength to lift an entire culture.

"When I moved to Long Beach [California] I'd draw and doodle my own flyers," she says. " 'Free lessons! Every Saturday. Meet me at the bottom of Junipero Hill. Learn how to go forward, backward, turn, stop, and go off a curb.' I'd make sixty or so copies and then go skate around handing them out. Pretty soon lessons were filling the parking lot with twenty to forty roller skaters every weekend. The power of giving something away for free is the best! It brings connection and community."

Michelle knew that the traditional roller-skating industry, even the other action sports industries, were not going to help at this point, so it was do-or-die. "There's the skateboarding industry that is very similar to roller-skating," Michelle says, "and if the women want to be that, then we have to see how they did and do it for ourselves. It's not a man/woman thing, but nowadays ninety percent of roller skaters are women. So roller-skating is essentially the flip side of skateboarding regarding gender participation."

Michelle strikes me as sensitive and shy, but she had forced herself into the "no choice" zone where she'd face repeated rejection handing out flyers to complete strangers. Look at it from a more conventional angle—a college-educated woman making clearly amateur pamphlets and roller-skating around to try and get people to play with her?

This is what we mean when we talk about the strength to be different. The ability not to give up, not to conform, not to kowtow to established

"experts" and their opinions, to continually take the emotional, social, maybe even physical beatings will reveal itself as strength, but only at a later reflective point. In the moment be prepared to feel like a wimpy failure as you struggle to lift the wrecked car and rescue a passion that few others want to save.

"There was a thing about making your own stuff," Shepard says, "creative repurposing of vintage clothes and making your own stencils and your own stickers. My parents were notoriously frugal, and so while all the kids at my school were into wearing Izod and Polo and Gant shirts, my parents got me the Sears knockoff shit. I knew there was no social future for me in that, but I could subvert the paradigm by making my own shirts. This is stuff that I can do and this is stuff that people from this new world respond to. All this time I had been drawing and painting and embarrassed to share it—now all of a sudden, I have a use for it that would work for something I'm passionate about."

Sometimes the mainstream tries to discourage deviation so strongly that it inadvertently spotlights willful divergence as a sign of strength. "Working *within* limitations helped create a style," Shepard says of the flair accompanying the expression of this kind of verve. "The sense of empowerment was incredible."

16

Find Your Flukes

t's no wonder misfits seem allergic to cookie-cutter self-help books that promote off-the-shelf success. For starters, any outcast knows there isn't a unicorn one-size-fits-all version of success. Just like everything else we're talking about—you have to DIY that concept yourself.

For a misfit, the idea of calculating a known career path can come off as absurd. "I can promise you, none of this shit was planned," Sacha told me repeatedly when prompted to reverse-engineer his life. These misfits have goals, but no reliable map to get there. What they do have is a technique of putting themselves into spontaneous circumstances and then trusting they'll make the necessary discoveries as they solve problems.

"When I put myself in uncertain situations, where I'm scared and uncomfortable and uncertain if I'm ever going to pull this thing off, I end up exposing myself, both my flaws and my strengths," Stacy says. "I end up doing something better than I could have otherwise. It's doing a detour around my brain to get directly into my heart. In order to do that, though, I have to be willing to be in these uncomfortable situations."

Now, the expected reaction would be to assume that repeated experiences like this would build confidence, an alpha ego assured of its conquering abilities, killer of self-doubt, vanquisher of fear. But it's much more complex and dynamic than that. *Where* that confidence lies is the misleading part. "I'm afraid of everything," Stacy says, "but I've come to realize that my greatest asset is recognizing that I am afraid of everything and I'm still going headfirst into things I'm afraid of. That's what has given me the life that I have. Living a life like that has kept me incredibly young, because that's the way I was when I was young—constantly living in a state of uncertainty, unsure whether I could do what I wanted to do."

Dang, misfits can't even be straightforward and conventional with the concept of strength and courage. "There's research that discovered that when you allow yourself to remain in an uncertain state, what it does is it shatters rigid neuronal pathways and makes way for positive neuronal pathways to be built in your brain," Stacy says. "So, you're actually breaking yourself down and building yourself back up simultaneously— that's the value of being in these uncertain situations, and I've come to realize that this is the only way to live. Even at this age, I keep putting myself in uncertain situations of learning things that are difficult, because I've found that's what lights my brain up."

Misfits who have achieved their own version of success intuitively knew what the dudes in white lab coats discovered with various hysterical strength experiments—one cannot activate it with intention no matter how maxed alpha male you go at it from. In a BBC article on the subject, E. Paul Zehr, a professor of neuroscience and kinesiology, essentially said that hysterical strength can't be processed, packaged, and bought off the shelf. One must be in a critical situation to unconsciously activate it. "You can't really design an experiment to do this in a lab and make people think they're going to die," he says. "Something has to happen by fluke."

Traditional society is all about replicating lab results. Go to school, get these grades, check these boxes, buy into this program, this belief

system, this version of success and you will attain a predictable result. Perform the cycle like so many lab rats before you. If anything, that process seems designed to keep your hidden strengths hidden. Misfits, on the other hand, flee the lab and subsequently train themselves to be open and reactive to flukes.

A "fluke" is defined as "an unlikely chance occurrence," and that sums up a great many misfit experiences considering our untemplated lifestyle. If you're like Mark, who seems addicted to pushing further and further into the uncertainty and nudging chance occurrences, then life has a way of presenting as a hurricane of fluky winds.

Before they had developed a fan base, DEVO was unable to generate any interest from major record labels, but Mark discovered that superstar rocker David Bowie was secretly playing backup for a punk singer.

"We knew David Bowie was playing keyboards for Iggy Pop, and Iggy was playing Cleveland," Mark says. "We had a pretty girl who was a friend of ours and gave her a demo tape and asked her to get backstage and give David the tape. She did, and the way Iggy tells it is that later on he and David were staying in Berlin, where the radio stations were not that good at the time, so they'd taken a suitcase of demo tapes that had been given to them. They picked one with an odd picture on it and start laughing as it played, not believing that it was a real band."

Back in North America, even people who knew better didn't always consider DEVO a real band. With no manager to book shows and hometown hatred so high that no venue would book them twice, DEVO was an unmitigated failure compared to a traditional band. DEVO had to leave the lab. New York City, a zip code much more encouraging and appreciative of freaks, was five hundred miles away. They borrowed a van that performed double duty as transport and mobile sleeping quarters.

Arriving in NYC, Jerry put on his best traditionalist costume and presented himself as DEVO's manager at the infamous Max's Kansas City, home to underground alternative groups like the Velvet Underground. Complete with briefcase stocked full of gig pamphlets and a self-financed EP, Jerry secured a gig. From the nightclub's POV, it seemed that DEVO was freaky enough to garner some attention regardless of how their music went over.

DEVO promised a set unlike anything anybody had seen before, even in the creative punk gutters of New York City. "We'd go to the library in Akron, Ohio, and rent a sixteen-millimeter projector that we'd take with us to New York's Max's Kansas City and CBGB," Mark says. "Before the show we'd set it on a table, hang a sheet on stage, and show this film to start the show. We had made our own films that showed us at a factory at quitting time where we were driving away and it looked like we were going to a show and then we'd take down the sheet and appear

on stage in the same outfits, which would eventually be torn apart during the show. Somehow, even in those punk clubs, the projector was never wrecked, and then we'd drive back home and return it to the library before incurring any late fees."

Punks photocopied DIY gig posters on standard-sized paper and plastered them around NYC for publicity. Mark, with his after-hours printing experience at Kent State, knew that he could get architecture blueprinting shops to cheaply produce movie-sized posters of DEVO in their hazmat suits posing with factory-looking dials and wheels. The posters faded quickly, but DEVO only needed them to last for the upcoming show. The renegade blueprint approach not only drew attention due to the irregular sizing—it made DEVO appear even more uncommon, because they weren't holding instruments. Pedestrians were often unsure of what to make of the strange piece of propaganda in front of them. "It did not look like a band at all," Mark says.

Bowie happened to be in NYC promoting his album *Heroes* and heard about the singular band playing at Max's. Iggy later told Mark that he and Bowie were such fans of their unique sonic bafflement that they started learning DEVO songs from the tape. "The first time I met Iggy he started singing 'Uncontrollable Urge' to me," Mark says.

Bowie caught a small set at Max's and became so enthused that, despite being one of the most famous rock stars in the world, he volunteered to introduce them for the following show. In a matter of days, a pack of struggling weirdos went from leaving Ohio with a public library projector showing homemade films cast with family members to being helped by one of the most popular freaks in the world. Bowie walked out on stage with a mic and enthusiastically said, "They are the de-evolution band: DEVO!"

Bowie continued introducing them the following night. When the Starman himself, an interstellar misfit star of the highest order who created an androgynous alien stage persona and wrote hit songs about astronauts lost in space, calls you the "band of the future" while paradoxically describing you as the de-evolution band? Outcasts on this planet, ones who feel like aliens themselves, listen.

"Artists are always looking for something interesting and new," Mark says. Does anybody think a traditional band manager would suggest wearing plastic hair, 3-D glasses, dressing in and then destroying hazmat suits, and testing the audience with subversive messages as a positive? No. There were no lab results, no proof that this approach connected to anybody, but DEVO projected a clear reflection of their outcast nature and misfits recognized the rare authenticity.

If DEVO hadn't dove into uncertainty and reacted as only they were capable of with a show of creative hysterical strength, if they had instead followed the instructions and imitated something popular, they would not have attracted Bowie. "Record company executives are always trying to find something that sounds like the last successful thing," Mark says, laying out the habit of traditionalists. " 'Just do it again so we can sell it again—we know how to sell that. We don't know how to sell something new.' "

With no support from an industry afraid to try to sell something new, the band that would help usher in the music world's New Wave DIY'd their dreams into existence. Tony recognizes this approach: "You were just making it happen . . . no one had a guidebook." In other words, taking advantage of a fluke: an unlikely chance occurrence.

"It was like a dream," Mark later told *NME* magazine. "We went from being penalized and attacked for writing original material in Ohio, because people there only wanted to see cover bands play, to the other extreme of working with Eno and Bowie."

No guerrilla techniques to get a demo tape into Bowie's hand, no making their own weird films and costumes, no budget PBJ-fueled five-

hundred-mile drives, no impersonating professional managers, no . . . searching for flukes, and DEVO would have died a quiet death in Ohio.

Survival. No choice. Individuality do-or-die. Hyperbolic? I'd argue that looking at how we react, how we push ourselves into the uncertain zone seeking flukes, there are high emotional and spiritual stakes in play that justify using those words. "I'm not training to gain confidence," Stacy says, well aware of the discovery that lies within the solution when one paints oneself into a corner. "I'm training myself to continually embrace uncertainty."

DEVO could have continued playing their music in regular clothes in Ohio, moaning about "nobody getting it" while waiting for somebody to discover them. Nobody was going to rescue them from stifling conformity, and they would have remained stuck and most likely depressed, instead of releasing an album that united misfits around the globe.

That album was cheekily called *Q: Are We Not Men? A: We Are DEVO!* which was advertised with the tagline "The Important Sound of Things Falling Apart" just to nudge listeners into the proper state of uncertainty.

EIGHT

BLOWBACK

Call the Exorcist

When a misfit passion mixes up the strength and excitement needed to deviate with intention, there will be the expected flak. People regularly dropped unsolicited advice regarding me wasting my life. Some openly found it embarrassing that I was obsessed with a childish loser activity. More than a few commented that I looked like "a queer" with my dyed hair. (This was considered an insult back then because . . . I guess gay people were infamous for cool progressive style?)

To all misfits at this point in the journey, this is fine. Better than fine. **When love of your misfit passion fortifies your palate, what used to taste like the bitter tang of rejection becomes a welcomed, delectable tart zing.** It is a delicious time of life when you embrace and find confidence and identity in being different.

But, like any recipe, precise measurement is vital.

By the time I was sixteen, I was sponsored by Powell-Peralta, the same skateboard brand that Tony Hawk rode for, and we had become friends. When I graduated high school at seventeen, I moved into his San Diego house. In California, skateboarding had increased in popularity and was everywhere. As with any incoming plague, biological or social, those in power began exerting measures to stop the infection. "No Skateboarding" signs became an expected part of urban land-scapes, school principals confiscated skateboards, "skate stoppers" were invented.

We were comfortable with a certain level of social rejection—we hadn't known anything else—but the heated anger accompanying this new overreaction was different. A misfit passion had mutated from a nuisance into a *threat*. At first news outlets had covered the popularity spike as a novelty—look at the wacky kids' new fad! But as the misfit reach spread and kids of conservative parents became interested in something traditional adults didn't understand, a dark paintbrush was used to slap a coat of danger over the activity. The colorful physical out-ward expression was now being linked to debilitating injuries, drug abuse, and antisocial behavior. It was deemed a gateway activity to lost lives.

This level of evil demands aggressive force to protect innocents. This realization hit me right in the chest as it was slammed into concrete and a knee went into my back and two arms forcibly put me in a choke hold.

Tony and I were at the Oceanside beach, slowly skating down a wide walkway where cyclists, beachgoers, and surfers casually flowed back and forth. It wasn't crowded as we casually rolled down a walkway like skaters had for years, not to mention that we were literally in the same area where the city had permitted annual skateboard contests.

Tony and I weren't doing tricks, blocking people, wiping out and in-advertently shooting our boards, we were killing time, literally going from point A to B, cruising with the flow of beachgoers, cyclists, and surfers, all of us moving at a leisurely pace. This colorful traffic was a celebrated part of the SoCal scenery, and nobody shot us dirty looks—well, nobody ex-cept a visibly uptight guy in oddly starched khaki shorts and a tucked-in blue golf shirt who shouted way too loudly at me to get off my board. This happened all the time, so I waved it off and forgot about it.

Then I heard the sound of running behind me and turned just in time to see said angry man lower his head to knock me off my board with a tackle. He landed on top of me on the concrete walkway and twisted me, putting his knees into my back as he pulled my shirt over my head before locking me up in a choke hold.

"Tell me that you're not going to fucking stop skating? Huh? Huh? Who's the tough guy now. Not so tough now, huh?"

He tightened his choke hold, and I started wheezing as he lifted me upright and began dragging me backward, my heels scraping the ground. This whole time he kept jerking and tightening the choke hold while repeatedly asking me who was the fucking tough guy. Was this a rhetorical question? Was it not clear to everyone by now that the wheezing guy in the choke hold being dragged backward was not the toughest. And how did I inadvertently enter a contest of male dominance? I was trying to skate *away* if anything.

Another identically dressed man ran up and apprehended Tony, who was not trying to flee but rather was frozen in place, wearing a perplexed look, trying to figure out what was happening. Turns out that these were two of the new beach cops, but they were not outfitted or dressed like police officers except for a small embroidered logo on their golf shirts. Beach Cop #1 dragged me backward—still choke-holding me as if I were a danger to all around—to the new portable police station/trailer. Once safely at the doorway he released his choke hold and pushed me inside.

The worst part was when the cop finally read aloud his little report saying how I had resisted arrest. Even though this was years ago, I can still hear him reading how "the officer politely asked him to step off his skateboard." Like an idiot I balked at this, but Tony shot me a look that said "Drop it, you're not going to win this," and I shut up as the cop

BLOWBACK

finished issuing us $275 tickets for skateboarding. The entire process was carried out with a calm that made it apparent that not only was this acceptable but that it was an appropriate reaction to a perceived threat.

Today, I think of this incident often as I watch people of all ages and stages of inebriation, rolling faster and more recklessly than any skater ever did, whizzing by on rented electric scooters. YouTube has montages of hapless scooter operators causing accidents, taking out pedestrians, smashing into walls and parked cars. I wonder if Beach Cop #1 or other social guardians are doing the old flying tackle on respectable middle-aged tourists speeding down beach pathways. But then again, I'm pretty sure riding a rental scooter never encouraged anyone to see the world differently, so it is much less dangerous.

To the misfit, it can be perplexing how unconventional activities, dress, and beliefs that don't harm anybody can be construed as dangerous. Aren't we simply making our own choices? We aren't forcing anybody to share our views, dye their hair the same color as ours, wear nail polish, participate in our passions. Just ignore us, kinda like you did before— you know, when you weren't targeting and bullying us.

History shows that traditional society has a low boiling point, and when a misfit activity heats up you'll notice the panic start percolating. There seems to be some sort of social gauge that detects when an outsider subculture grows from isolated stragglers to a flourishing active group of participants and supporters.

Therein lies the problem.

The inescapable, cruel paradox to this scenario is that the more successful we become at spreading our specific misfit vibe, the more successful we become at attracting reactionary attention. When an increasing number of people begin to collectively question the status quo, you will

see traditionalists first become extremely confused, and subsequently ignite an anger proportionate to that uncertainty.

We looked at how hysterical strength can help misfits push past self-doubt and lack of permission to DIY our lives. This, obviously, is awesome. That said, it's not as if hysteria in general, the kind that leads to widespread panic, favors misfits. If we're being honest about hysteria, fanatical conformists really have a corner on the market. The mainstream whips hysteria into a frenzy with alarming speed, unleashing it like an army of attack dogs.

One aspect of the status quo's collective attack that never fails to disgust is how the bullies, the persecutors, twist themselves into the injured party. There is a seed of martyrdom, as if we, the misfits, forced their hand. It's *our* fault that we made their lives so fraught with danger. We became so dangerous that the only reasonable reaction was to attack us with extreme viciousness.

To absolve the panicked conformist of any reasonable self-reflection, you'll notice that a handy narrative is employed: "Hey, deviant, this is your fault—you were the one that chose to present a threat, therefore, any overreaction is not only defensible but warranted." Aka: "You started it!" Remember the school coach's passing commentary to the bullies dragging Mark into the bathroom? "Mothersbaugh, you bring it on yourself."

While strident conformists may be wired for hysteria, most of the general public isn't inclined to panic so easily. For the guardian of the status quo, this presents a problem. When you can't get people off the sofa, how do you chase the monster out of the village? Well, there's a tried-and-true persecution tool guaranteed to scare the bejesus out of everyone and sever any empathy: demonization.

Being different can very easily ferment into being perceived as evil with the right amount of demonization. Gay people are going to hell.

Heavy metal bands backmask—play backward—Satanic suicide messages on their albums. Punk music and skateboarding are gateways to drug abuse and self-mutilation. Drag queens groom children. Beyond the binary are faking to perv out in bathroom stalls. Hip-hop artists are drug-dealing thugs.

But if we're looking for a highwater mark of modern conformist hysteria, then we need to revisit the "satanic panic" of the 1980s that targeted Dungeons & Dragons and spiraled into total cultural insanity.

Back before nerds decided to own the world, they were generally considered social bottom feeders, subject to demeaning stereotypes. One being that they escaped reality by getting lost in geeky worlds removed from "real life."

Being a sci-fi nerd was understandable—*Star Trek* had been on mainstream TV and boomers understood the lure—but when a new type of imaginative fantasy board game became increasingly popular, one that was richly complicated with worldbuilding, actively placing the player into a highly immersive imaginative world with a variety of fantastical outcomes? Conformists became very confused, and then some of them, naturally, became very angry.

"Dungeons & Dragons and other role-playing games allow people to create characters that are more like they want to be, and as such learn the steps they can take to go in that direction and create somebody entirely different from who they are," Matt Mercer of Critical Role, a group that plays the game online, said in a YouTube video. What could be wrong with that? One might even argue that many parents already do this when they make children wear suits and ties and dress shoes.

The imaginative empowerment of Dungeons & Dragons sounds healthy. Dr. Jon, who started the Brooklyn Strategist board game shop, told me how getting involved in D&D gave him "amazing emotional and cognitive rewards that no board game had given me before," and he was not alone. D&D became a cultural phenomenon. Dr. Jon, like millions of other kids, would excitedly gather with friends and spend hours at a table laughing and screaming in excitement as they adventured through an interactive and imaginative campaign together.

Then a private investigator was hired to search for a missing kid and discovered that the student had played this newfangled game called Dungeons & Dragons. Trying to solve the case, the investigation put a focus on something the investigator and police didn't understand—the concept of this new game—and voila, we had a hypothesis that garnered national attention. Along with the police briefings, newspapers came up with helpful headlines like "Game Might Have Turned into Deathtrap," "Fantasy Game Death Feared," "Did Dragons, Dungeons Swallow Dallas Egbert?" All printed in oversized bold fonts and delivered right to your doorstep.

In a *NYT* video about satanic panic, the private investigator who searched for the missing kid demonstrates the mainstream's hysterical approach to things that scare them. "You're leaving the world of reality into the world of fantasy. It advocated murder, decapitation . . . and I'm going, this isn't a healthy game. How can it be a healthy game?"

This kind of hysterical sensationalism creates such an uproar that it can plant seeds in well-meaning parents' minds. At the same time that Dr. Jon was discovering the joys of this new type of game, his parents "became very concerned because there were reports of D&D being part of the occult. Without truly understanding what it was, my parents were very worried that I was falling into a cult of some sort."

At least Dr. Jon didn't have the type of parents who simply burned their kids' D&D sets. Although, D&D cocreator Gary Gygax was informed that this method of disposal was ineffective. "Somebody said they threw their copy of Dungeons & Dragons into the fire and it screamed," he said in a vintage news piece.

"I can laugh about it now," Dr. Jon says, "but at some point my parents brought me to a family psychologist. I sat down in the first session and they talked about the concern over the game. I remember explaining what the game was and toward the end of the session the psychologist looked at me and said, 'Jon has a very clear understanding of what is real, what isn't real, that this is a game, and this isn't something that is happening in reality,' and promptly kicked me out of the session and met with my parents the rest of the time and I was never invited back."

Demonization was such a successful strategy that for a while it became a bit of a one-devil-fits-all-misfit vibe. Heavy metal was a newly popular aggressive genre of music, and some of the most popular bands were hauled in front of Congress to testify, to prove that they weren't trying to drag society into hell. Judas Priest was even taken to court in a "subliminal message trial" for supposedly hiding suicidal messages in their lyrics. I still have a 1980s newspaper clipping of an Ohio community confused by graffiti of "Rat Bones," the same image Stecyk created that derailed my life in such a beautiful way. The headline? "Satanic Cult Worship Concerns Local Police."

Many demonized jewels are bedazzled all over the article, but this one provides the gist: "This bizarre looking symbol and 'BONES' found spray-painted onto a culvert in Munson Township . . . is the work of a Satanic cult, according to local authorities, and is only one example of serious potentially dangerous devil worship."

The police chief quoted in the article had reportedly attended "educational seminars" on Satanic cults—a booming industry for authority figures in the 1980s. "I want parents to simply be aware of the possibility and to have an idea of what to look for," the chief said. The paper added, "He said the cults tend to attract teenagers."

It's funny until you meet a kid whose parents bought into this vibe

and forbade their child from skateboarding or hanging out with friends who played Dungeons & Dragons or listened to heavy metal music. In that sense, conformist mission accomplished. When national newscasters say, "There is no doubt that teenage Satanic activity in this country is increasing dramatically" over images of a punk or metal mosh pit at a concert, we see how dysfunction once again unites misfits, this time through negative profiling.

The real evil of this technique is how it whips people into such a panic that it impedes any reasonable discussion or exchange of ideas. Luckily, like most mainstream fashions, the Satan-is-gonna-get-ya fad died out and outcast communities continued doing what they have always done—creating a sense of belonging for castaways.

In a YouTube piece on Dungeons & Dragons, a player bravely shares his very un-Satanic experience with that community. "Everybody kept downgrading me, telling me I was worthless, useless . . . I didn't know where to go with my life and I thought to myself that I was just going to end it all. But my best friend recommended I go see Critical Role and see what they do. It started making sense and made me happy and started to make me think about what I can do. Instead of saying, 'I can't' it says, 'How can I change my life?' And because of that, I'm here today and I'm enjoying the holy crap out of myself."

In a 1980s news report, Gary Gygax laid out the vacation from conventionality that games like his provide. "All of us at times feel a little inadequate in dealing with the modern world. It would feel much better if we knew we were superheroes or a mighty wizard."

I've never imagined myself as a wizard, but I'll look at a paved bank behind a paint store and behold it transforming into an area of unimaginable fun and challenge that remains invisible to non-skaters. Mark has composed music out of purposely broken musical equipment that makes people smile and dance together. Seneca takes a blank page and stirs up awe and emotions and connection in strangers. Dr. Jon has created a portal at The Brooklyn Strategist where anybody considered weird feels welcomed. Michelle fastens wheels to feet and makes you feel like you're flying. I never thought about it that way, but sure, all of this might just be some kind of misfit magic.

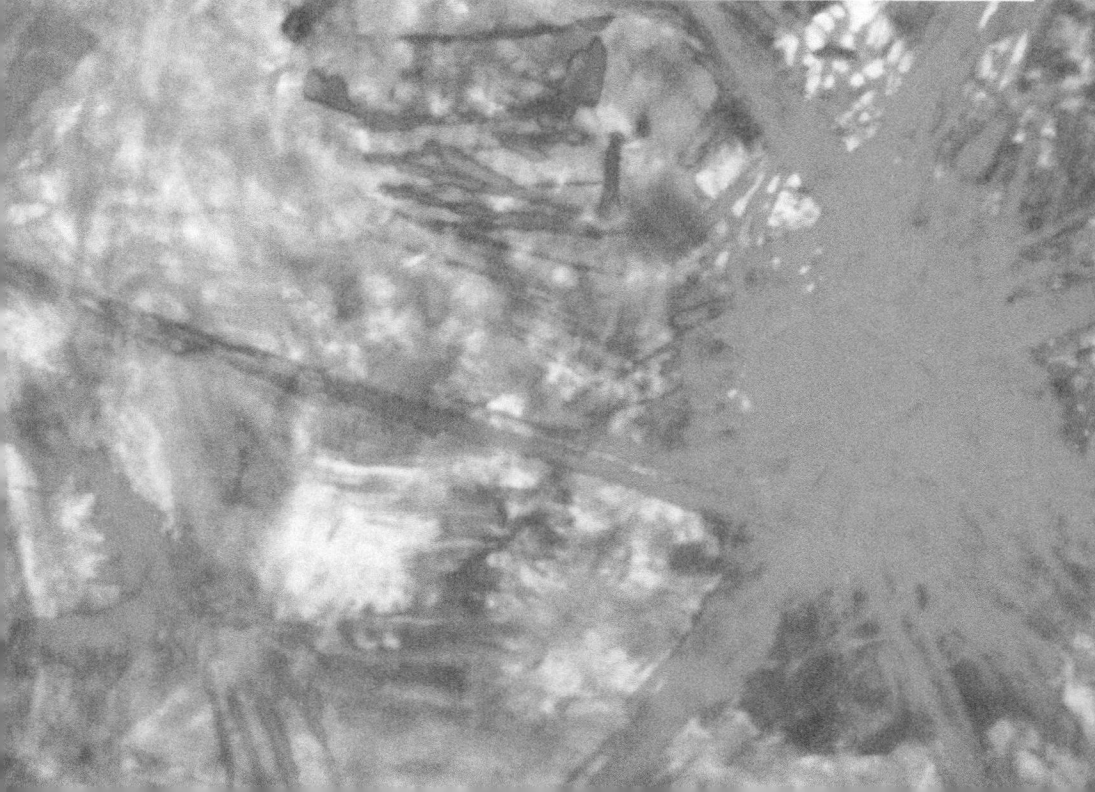

SHEPARD FAIREY "First you trust that adults know what they're talking about, and then you question that a bit as a teenager, but then you understand that what they decide has merit and value and what they think has virtuosity is very arbitrary in a lot of ways.

"The idea with OBEY is that people usually obey very subconsciously, and that is how propagandists and manipulators operate: They make you think it was your idea to follow the agenda they wanted you to follow. The idea was to make people confront obedience consciously, even if they think, *Obey? Obey what?* Exactly. What do you submit to? What do you subscribe to?"

NINE

OUT OF THE
SHADOWS

18

Cup o' Shit

In the famous short horror story "The Monkey's Paw," a mummified primate paw grants wishes, and while they end up coming true, a horrifying unforeseen price is extracted. A couple wishes for two hundred bucks (it's a *very* old story) and receives it as compensation after their son dies. Then they wish for the son to come back and realize too late that he will literally return having crawled out of his grave.

Any marginalized outsider who has endured bullying, systematic persecution, or cultural minimization is familiar with the wish to be accepted, celebrated, valued as who they are. It's also natural to want to share the joy our misfit passions awakened so that fellow fringe dwellers can experience it for themselves. I can still remember the fanatical rants Kevin spewed in 1985 as we drove around in his dented Pinto getting kicked out of places for skateboarding. "I mean, come on, professional *bowlers* make way more money than pro skaters, and they bowl on TV! How can you not see how much radder skating is than bowling? Can you *imagine* if skating was as popular as bowling, how many lives that would change?"

My misfit passion had exploded in popularity by the latter part of the

1980s. Skateboard pros cashed $20,000 monthly royalty checks and a subversive DIY ecosystem including media, distributions, and competition was brought to life.

The beautiful part was how a bold cultural fence line continued to divide the mainstream and our subculture. This was a misfit golden age as a fringe subculture remained cryptic to the general public, yet flourished culturally and economically—a world for skaters by skaters. It wasn't until 1995 that the non-skating mainstream became seriously involved with ESPN's X Games, and boy oh boy was there a price to be paid, which often seems the case when a misfit wish is granted.

Let me use a cup of human shit to illustrate.

In 1987 I was a full-on skateboard freak, part of a tight community of rejects in Vancouver. I skated hours every day and worked at Kevin's back-alley DIY skatepark, which was simply a warehouse filled with wooden ramps. The place reeked with passionate notes of dust and wood, aged sweaty pads, and funky bacteria, all wafting together into the noses of skaters for one of the most beautiful scents—the smell of belonging.

I remember one evening well. The Richmond Skate Ranch closed at nine, and not yet driving, I had to skate through an industrial area to the closest bus stop. I rolled past the open weedy fields and the stark concrete warehouses, down the dimly lit, deserted streets, and was about to exit the industrial area into a well-lit, busier street.

A teeny older-model Honda Civic drove down the dark street behind me, noticeable because hardly anybody used these roads at this time of night. Slowing to a stop, the two passenger-side windows rolled down to reveal five large jocks, all in Richmond High jock jackets. Old Civics were crazy small and the contents were so big and sardined that the whole deal gave off a clown car vibe, but these were also the type known to pick fights with skaters.

The synchronized window roll-down made my skater sense tingle, so

I stopped, kicked my board up into my hands, and checked the field behind me, pretty sure I could lose them if I got a good start running. Worst-case scenario, you start swinging your board. They didn't look ready to get out, though. The passenger in the front still had his seat belt on and the jock seated behind him was beginning to lean out the window instead of opening the door.

"Hey, man, do you know where—"

He raised a hidden Big Gulp cup up over the windowsill and threw it at me. Even as I dodged the main splash, the unmistakable scent announced the digestive origins of the brown liquid chunked with human waste. Laughing, they tried to peel out, but the low horsepower and heavy contents reduced the getaway to a very gradual acceleration.

I craned my neck to get as far away from myself as possible and held my breath as I crossed the street to a ditch, dunking my shirt into less personalized stink water coated with an oily green film. After sponging my pants I twisted my shirt dry and pulled it over my head, smelling like a slightly less repulsive combination of organic decay.

The bus driver opened the door and shook his head. "C'mon, man, I didn't shit myself!" I pleaded. "I'm not drunk. Some jocks threw a cup o' shit on me. I don't even drink. I rinsed off in a ditch. I'll sit at the back so you won't smell me." We always sat at the back anyway and I was also pretty sure he had to let me on, my being a minor and all.

Luckily, my parents were already asleep so I didn't have to explain. I showered, put my clothes in a plastic bag, twisted the top, and buried it in the outside trash with my board, which was now cursed with jock-shit stains.

Setting up a new skateboard (as a sponsored skater I was sent boxes of free equipment) acted as a ritual that helped me process the event. There were no tears of frustration, no beating the pillow wondering, "Why me?" The thoughts racing around my mind trying to find an exit

OUT OF THE SHADOWS

ramp centered on how the jocks filled the cup. "Was it communal? How does one schedule shits? Were laxatives involved? How long did they drive around in a car perfumed with their own poop? Was there spillage? How do brains like theirs work?"

Was I bummed that five humans had picked me to throw their shit on? Well, yeah, but it didn't register as a *completely* negative incident. Did I think these jocks drove around looking for a skateboarder, for me specifically? No, I'm pretty sure they drove around searching for somebody *different,* a person presenting as a minority fringe dweller, an identifiable "loser."

There is clarity when somebody throws their own shit on you. The fecal flingers were the exact people I did *not* want to become. In the DEVO documentary, there's footage of one of the very unconventional band's early gigs in an Ohio bar frequented by hard-bitten factory workers. Even watching it through a pixelated screen, the menace with which the audience expecting cookie-cutter rock and roll yells "Fuck you!" and "Fuck yourselves!" still makes you anxious for the band.

I don't think the seasoned misfit ever embraces these volatile reactions, but we do learn an outsider alchemy that converts aggressive reactions into fuel. "It kinda energized us when we were rejected that way," Mark's bandmate Jerry says in the doc. **It made us stronger. We thought, *if those assholes don't like us then we know we're doing the right thing.*"**

"I had several arrests for skateboarding and fireworks before any of my street art arrests," Shepard says, like many misfits using experiences of traditional overreactions as a report card of sorts to share. "I don't even count them. I've had eighteen street art arrests."

"Getting caught was part of it," Roger says of his early graffiti days. "You've got friends who have been caught, maybe you've been caught, chased by the police, but any skateboarder, punk-rock kid has probably been chased by the police for doing something at some point. It shapes you."

A friend once told me, "In high school, during gym class, a few guys held me down and said, 'Tell us punk sucks.' It was the stupidest thing on earth. I thought, *It's so rad that you guys are so annoyed.* But I wasn't going to say it, so they punched me."

When my friends bandy around confrontation stories, the cup o' shit or being tackled by a cop are so relatable and common that they don't even stand out. **Some people collect Star Wars figures or stamps. Misfits collect hostile rejections.**

TONY HAWK "If I'm at an event in a group full of mainstream athletes and legends, I'm always like, 'What am I doing here? This is crazy.' We weren't revered like that and nor do we want to be. What we do is so subjective, and so when you say, 'That's the best skater!' 'That skater is better than that one,' it's just . . . what are you talking about? It's all apples to oranges. We all do our own thing. We all have our own style. We all have our sense of community because of it. We respect each other's differences, strengths, and even weaknesses or whatever."

On top of overreactions, another tricky part of misfit progression is that the more successful we become at growing our subcultures the more attention we draw to ourselves from the culture vultures. Commodifiers have long practiced the capitalist art of taking a culture's raw materials and processing them into something plastic and sellable. When John Lydon was with the Sex Pistols, he went from being chased and beat up by strangers and demonized for his revolutionary attitude to having an unwanted front-row seat in a new fashion trend as the punk scene turned into a costumed fad available off the shelf.

"They became merely copyists, and that's not very good at all," John, aka Johnny Rotten, said on a talk show. If you look at early punk, you'll see an explosion of thrifty creativity and unique shock styles, but once the culture became popular a uniformity seeped into the development. "The punk ethic became a punk uniform," Johnny said. "You're not in the music game to join the army. People don't respect individuality enough, and everybody should have their own personality and to hell with competition."

"Just because you're in a punk or hardcore band doesn't mean that you're authentic," Roger says, "that you aren't just a follower of one of the others."

True individuality can't be sold—that type of motivation kills it on contact. Irregular, awkward, and uncomfortable edges are always shaved off when square pegs are hammered through round production holes. But the idea that you can buy something mass-produced that supposedly says you are an individual? That's printing money. **The true art of commodification is providing the comfort of a round peg while encouraging the belief that you are a square peg.**

I attended many skateboard contests in the 1980s, and everyone there was part of the fringe. There were impromptu mosh pits when sticker and board tosses started. Punk bands played. Old cars were skated on and smashed up as part of the contest. Cops occasionally arrested competitors on contest sites.

A skater might not come in first, yet still "win" the contest by landing a memorable trick. Stacy once promoted a pro skater on the basis of his

talent for "losing" contests. But in 1995 the X Games arrived. The X Games sold the renegade image of alternative sports by hammering them into familiar sports templates and directing all the focus on winners and losers like traditional championships. Technically, they were both "contests," but one celebrated a traditional winner-take-all while the other intuitively celebrated the culture through a highly idiosyncratic form of progression.

To tell the truth, I wasn't thinking too hard about the impact of somebody outside of skating putting on a televised contest in 1995. I didn't imagine it becoming a success because they had a bungee-jumping contest alongside skateboarding. It was cool seeing my friends receiving exposure on a national television channel, but then at a later contest I looked around and saw the expected fringe lunatics mixed in with people who looked like the guys that threw their shit on me, and the disorientation threw me into a type of social vertigo.

But, wait a sec . . . Isn't that what so many of us wished for at some point, that our weirdo passion would gain exposure and become celebrated? As a kid, I had stumbled around aimlessly for years until *Back to the Future* randomly clued me into skateboarding and now people all over the world would be exposed to elite skateboarding in their living rooms.

I didn't want to be dodging cups o' shit for the rest of my life. I didn't want you doing that either. I wanted more people to experience dynamic freedom within themselves that a misfit passion unlocks. What was the best way to accomplish that mission? Was there only one way? These are the uncomfortable moments when something that means so much to so few begins to mean so much less to so many more. How does this work? What do we gain and lose in this transaction?

Stupid monkey paw.

STACY PERALTA "I don't know how well the general public can really relate to you as a skater or surfer. They still don't understand what we do. In the surfing world you suddenly had all these big-time clothing companies like Quiksilver and Billabong and you had competitive circuits and structure and champions—those are the ways that people have the mediums to look into surfing, but they're still not getting it because those things have nothing to do with surfing.

"They are just a structure that lets you look into it, but it's not what it is about. That's the thing—we sometimes forget that. Skateboarding has nothing to do with contests or manufacturers, skateboarding has to do with whoever gets on a board and starts riding down a hill. That's it. That's what it is. All the other stuff is structure, and it gives us the illusion that we understand these things better, but you can only understand it when you get on it and do it. Putting on Quiksilver clothes gives people the illusion that they're a surfer because they're wearing surf trunks and surf shirts and walking barefoot."

19

The Jujitsu of Selling Out

We all love our weirdo passions, but when they start growing beyond perimeters it becomes much more complex to control the growth. Perhaps that's by design? Is it good to have that much control over your subculture? Is there a danger of people in positions of power throttling progression to stay in their heightened positions? "People would tell me, 'Well, that's not how you do it,'" Shepard remembers. "That was a joke I made from the beginning: Graffiti was all about rule breaking for a little while, and now it's imposed all these rules on itself?"

So how are we supposed to protect what is authentic to our cherished subculture from the capitalist vampires? What is exclusion and what is protection when what was a hidden doorway now requires members to stand guard? "A belief in authenticity can be what's driving it," Shepard says, "but because what is authentic is constantly evolving that can't be a rearview-mirror thing. **I always feel that the least creative people are the ones who want to police what a culture is supposed to look like, sound like. The creative people are saying, 'No. What is exciting about this is the free space to keep moving, redefining.'**"

In a Dungeons & Dragons documentary on YouTube, not looking geeky enough shows how overprotection of a misfit culture turns into aggressive conformity. "There will always be gatekeepers, people trying to control the 'purity' of the game," a female player says. "There definitely was a culture of 'This was my safe space when I was trying to get away from those people, and now those people are in my safe space.'"

But that safe space that we found in our misfit passion's community has to adapt to the mainstream pressure around it. It's seductively easy to turn safe spaces into panic rooms where you try to lock the doors from the inside to keep change out.

Early on, Tony was mocked for selling out skateboarding. The name-callers assumed he was trading something private and precious for generic mainstream currency. But he's a smart dude and recognized that a power shift was available. "The X Games needed Tony as much as Tony needed them to make the 900 happen," Stacy says of the most famous alternative sporting moment in history, one that changed how the world perceived sports, not just skateboarding. "They both needed each other."

"At some point, the tide turned," Tony says. "We knew we had established ourselves here. Kids like skateboarding now, networks like skateboarding now, and some people were still presenting it wrong. They didn't skate, they didn't care, and they thought they knew better, that they could just grab a couple of elements of it—aesthetics, looks, language—and combine it with a Madison Ave approach and that's all it took. At some point, that shit didn't fly, because kids got privy, they got savvy. And then endemic companies came on the rise and they flourished because they were authentic."

By the time the Olympics began sniffing around skateboarding to draw in younger demographics, the power dynamics had shifted. Tony was on an NPR program as an unofficial ambassador of skateboarding, and said bluntly, "I feel like the Olympics needs skateboarding's 'cool factor' more than skateboarding needs their validation."

By this time, Tony had used all of his newfound mainstream popularity to create vehicles that more accurately conveyed his misfit passion, the most successful being the *Tony Hawk's Pro Skater* series, which became one of the most successful video game franchises in history. In a misfit masterstroke, Tony circumvented the mainstream's presentation but used that newfound fame to immerse people in skating's subculture in their living rooms. He worked on every aspect of the game development, carefully included the right slang, and personally mixtaped the soundtrack so that millions of unassuming players around the world were exposed to Dead Kennedys and Agent Orange without having to randomly catch a video in a skate shop like Shepard or be gifted a punk cassette tape like Ed.

Tony worked on deals that afforded him more and more creative control as his popularity increased, and when he built up enough mainstream currency he spent it. "I was trying my best to represent skateboarding authentically, and there was always a lot of compromise," Tony says. "They listened to me, but weren't willing to go all the way with it. I was able to at least show skateboarding authentically, but when our video game became a huge success, there was no longer a compromise—it was either my final say or approval or we're not doing it."

You want to work with one of the world's most popular misfits? He's going to make sure his passion is presented authentically. It is a little-known fact, but as Tony was making millions of dollars in endorsement deals, he was writing into his contracts that mainstream sponsors had to pay into his nonprofit skatepark foundation, which has given over thirteen million dollars to help build over six hundred permanent skateparks in low-income areas all over the country so that people can be exposed to authentic skateboarding regardless of how the mainstream presents it.

TEN

THE DIZZINESS OF THE KOOK ZONE

20

Grow Up, Already

I t's important for the misfit to be healthy. Staying hydrated and getting enough sleep are important, as is exercising a little rebellion on the regular. One consistent observation throughout my life has been how highly conformist people appear so old and stiff. I'm not dealing in ageism here, because being a misfit has nothing to do with driver's license dates, but considering how often traditionalists call us "immature," I believe this may be a point of pride on their side.

The real youthful juice comes with maintaining an open curiosity, the same kind that led you to your misfit passion.

One time I was driving with Stacy and he asked how old I felt. He wasn't talking about how many calendars I'd blown past, he meant at what part of my life did energy manifest in a way that made me feel most alive and active. And if I'd found a way to keep that as a gravitational center for life. "Seventeen," I said. "But like a seventeen without a driver's license."

He nodded. "Yeah, I still feel sixteen. I still feel like I'm getting up and discovering things all day."

One of the most powerful dismissals of misfits and their activities is the "immature" label. Unlike "adults" who purposely put governors on their imagination, we're rolling dice, shuffling cards, and imagining ourselves as wizards and warlocks battling armies of the undead. We're mischievously climbing fences to draw on walls like naughty kids instead of perfecting real art, according to them. We're oversharing through music and writing. We're still chasing the adrenaline kick that ragamuffins get from jumping bikes off curb cuts and dirt jumps—will I crash or not? We're acting weird for attention.

For misfits embracing that curiosity it can be tricky to know what the rules are, why wanting an occupation playing UNO is deemed silly, but poker is an admirable, televised profession. Buckle up leather chaps, droop a chain wallet, wear a skull face mask, and drive around on a Harley for the weekend? Perfectly acceptable form of cosplay. Put on chain metal and go to a Renaissance fair? Ahem . . . we have a problem. The mainstream, of course, is in charge of designating the "toy" label, and we are told that there comes a time when you must put away your toys and enter the real world: You must "grow up."

There was a world champion in a misfit passion whose dad was such a hardcore traditionalist that he treated his child's misfit passion like a pus-filled zit needing to be lanced. **"Get this shit out of your system, because you are going to have to enter the real world and you won't know what hit you."**

What "real" world is that? And where is the unreal one? The why-don't-you-grow-up and not-ready-for-the-real-world insults pave a prejudiced bias that the free-form skills we develop as kids, as immature outcasts, have no redeeming value in real-world adulthood. To act like an adult is to follow a strict code of conduct.

My old skate buddy Kevin was arrested once for starting a riot at a skateboard demo in the late '80s. The reality was that the tour van broke

down and the pros arrived late, but by then the police were already aggressively trying to disperse the crowd and it was their overreaction creating chaos. The pro skaters were arrested upon arrival and taken to the police station, where other cops rotated in to get some practice with their insults. "Who'd want to watch a bunch of drug addicts like you skateboard?" And then the expected "Aren't you losers a bit too old for a kiddie thing like skateboarding?"

Kevin knew how this type of brain worked, and pointed to a fellow pro skater. "Just so you know—what this guy makes in annual royalties is more than you three make combined in a year." The cops had no more insults after that exchange. Apparently, for conformists to this particular culture, money kills "immaturity" on contact.

Fun Fact: This misfit world champion proved to be more measurably ready for the "real world" than his father using "real world" metrics. The company that he cofounded to celebrate his outsider passion was sold for twenty million dollars.

STACY PERALTA: "We're told that we have to become adults and 'get our lives together,' but we're given this fallacy that growing up means you never screw up anymore, you're never weak anymore, you're never vulnerable anymore, which is a fallacy. You want to be in those places, in a position where you can experience yourself as a kook and not good at something for a while, because it opens up so many aspects of who you are and enables you to be sixteen years old again, when you were learning something.

"Think of how insecure we were when we learned new

> things. I encourage people to head straight for the insecu-
> rities, go full on into them, go into the weakness, into the
> frailness, because that's where you're going to find your
> strength, your greatness, and that's where life is going to
> be able to work its powers on you. It's taken everything
> that I've got to remain open to these experiences."

There seems to be a lot of buzz in traditional society about finding the right life balance. The act of shifting aspects of your life around to find a new balance appears to be treated as a transitional state, something to be completed before locking in a better life with a consistent steady balance.

For misfits, the formula is flipped, as we have a different history with instability and uncertainty—we know it as an oxygen-rich environment full of intense learning, an experience that we carefully cultivate. A famous philosopher once talked about "the dizziness of freedom," and that quote always stuck, because to misfits this is not a state to be avoided. I thought about the motivation behind the "immature" spinning around in circles that I did as a kid—trying to get wobbly on purpose, giggling with delight as I stumbled around trying to find balance. **There is a youthfulness, a joy of discovery, an education to be found in the action of disorientation and recovery.**

"I got up this morning and was so anxiety-ridden because I had to get in the water and try to get better at hydrofoil surfing," Stacy told me as he broke down his dizzying morning. "I took my dog out and checked the beach where I was going to go, and it looked perfect. I went home, got my stuff, went back to the beach . . . and all of a sudden the waves were big and it wasn't right. I got all freaked out and went to another beach—there were no waves there—and went to another beach and by then I had so much anxiety in me because I had to go out and do this thing. Had to."

Now, Stacy knows how to surf, skateboard, kiteboard—he could have chosen one of those activities, had fun, lessened his anxiety. But he wanted to feel sixteen again, gloriously immature and dizzy chasing a passion for no other reason than the joy it gave him. Well, that and the terror. "I was terrified to go out, because it was only my sixth time doing it and my first time alone and it's dangerous. I was wondering how much of my session was going to be falling and me actually riding and learning. All the time that I'm carrying my board to the beach, I'm nervous, fearful. But I had to do it."

From what I can tell from my weirdo perch, a lot of society's marketing for conventional maturity is about the supposed mastery of emotional flow, squashing the explosive uncertainty of pre-adulthood. The attraction is obvious. Understandably, anxiety gets a bad rap. Too much and it's a debilitating, relentless enemy. Not enough and there's depression, lack of identity, and an inflammatory fear of *any* anxiety on the horizon. Luckily, for misfits, the lack of an illusionary structure means that we're regularly in a kind of anxiety dojo, constantly working out new moves to deal with anxiety.

I have a wife and kids and a home. In the court of law, I am an adult. But none of that changes how I feel when I slide the tail of my skateboard over the coping and drop into a bowl and try to learn a new trick. There is a very personal equilibrium that I am constantly adjusting as I actively rebalance risk vs reward, purposely inviting anxiety into my life in a tempered manner. Yeah, I did need to have my ankle reconstructed a year ago and need to schedule an MRI for my shoulder as I write this, but that is part of my balance, which feels like I swallowed a delicious Roman candle when I do finally land a new trick or choose a career as a writer and try to sell a book that gets rejected until that one offbeat editor decides to take a chance. (Tony's autobiography was rejected by nineteen out of twenty publishers, but it went on to be a success.)

"I do love a good challenge," Seneca says of spending a life being dizzy. "There's pain and insecurity involved as part of the artistic process—we have to go through some discomfort. If you don't go through discomfort you're not evolving, you're not pushing yourself forward."

The beautiful part of being a misfit at this point in the cycle is that you have experience independently throttling various challenges, drives, and anxieties of life. The simple act of choosing to do an unstructured activity puts pressure on you from the start. A friend once explained the gravitational pull toward their alternative interest in a way that encompasses any and all of our passions: "You pick the stuff you want to do—like, I don't have to run to first base right now, I can run to third. I can go any direction I want." But packaged within the freedom to run in any direction you want comes the anxiety of making choices and dealing with unknown consequences. Herd mentality is marketed to solve this worry, which is why I'll highlight Mark's pointed lyrics in DEVO's song "Freedom of Choice": "Freedom of choice is what you got. Freedom *from* choice is what you want."

The anxiety from choice can prove to be wildly engaging, and with constant practice and a refined technique it will build confidence. "I don't want to live in a comfort zone," Tony says. "I don't want to live a life on repeat. I want to evolve. I want to keep getting better, because that's what I do through skating."

In the same way that skateboards originated from mischievous kids cutting up roller skates and nailing them onto planks of wood, misfits have the freedom to saw apart conventional adulthood and build something unauthorized with both mature and "immature" parts. There is no valid reason why having a sense of play, curiosity, absurd humor,

exploration, and excitement is somehow incompatible with being responsible.

There is a misfit humor, energy, and curiosity that is comparable to a youthful outlook, but when labeled as "immature" it arrives with the stigma that we can't handle the really serious responsibilities. I've even caught myself falling into the traps of this traditional stereotype. I worked on a project with a high-ranking person involved in politics and believed the hype, expecting a black-belt level of responsibility and efficiency from this person. Their life had been moving on such a stable set of tracks for so long in such a different way than mine that I assumed their version of "adulthood" would be at what the mainstream advertised as a "mastery" level.

This person was in the mainstream machine at the highest levels of adulthood, all the way to working in the White House, and I saw first-hand what a joke the adult version of responsibility can be. Sure, this person had a precision haircut and a closet full of tailored outfits, but they repeatedly missed deadlines, with seemingly no empathy or sense of concern. Whereas misfits I know who DIY'd their lives were acutely aware that if they didn't keep their shit tight, there would be no safety net when they F'd up. I was the one meeting deadlines, doing the work, showing up to meetings on time . . . and then heading off to play on my immature rolling toy.

The realization that traditional adulthood is a construct and NOT a single model is one of the best get-outta-jail cards we can give ourselves. There's a quote from a celebrated misfit that applies to all outcasts finding the dynamisms of life within an "immature" activity. Insert your specific passion on the blank line and see if it doesn't ring true. "You don't quit _____ because you got old, you got old because you quit _____."

21

What to Do When Hit by a Truck

aving surrounded myself with misfits for most of my life, there's a recognition of how a developed alternative approach and an unconventional community help solve problems in all aspects of life. Actually, I'll go one better—it can save your life.

There was nothing beyond a distant irritation of a slow tugging, annoyingly persistent, pulling me toward something, until a breaking of surface tension announced a new world, birthing sharp pain, confusion, disorientation, all of it shaking uncontrollably. There was light, impossibly bright, and a large vibrating face looming impossibly large.

This was not God, but merely a physician stitching my face up with no anesthesia in a trauma center. The shaking, I'd find out later, was surging adrenaline bouncing my body on the operating table, helping imprint the memory when all surrounding memories were being deleted into nothingness by traumatic brain damage. Luckily, it was a holiday, the afternoon after Christmas, sunny and warm in San Diego, so the incident by the beach had plenty of spectators.

Witness 1: "White Chevy Z71 truck driving north struck cyclist from behind. Speed unknown. The victim was launched into the air over the truck, did 1.5 flips and landed head to pavement."

Witness 2: "I was walking out to the street, heard a truck gas it. Then a boom followed by brakes being slammed on. As I looked up I saw a helmet in the middle of the street. The helmet was still rocking. I looked up the street and saw a man lying on the ground with fragments of the bike scattered."

An Instagrammer commented with more color. "Damn. This dude just got hit by a truck on his bike and flew over the car. Helmet 100 yrds 1 way an his bike 100 yrds the other. So crazy. I hope he's alright he was pretty jacked up."

There was a damage report. Fractured spine. Tendon damage. Face ripped. Nose broken. A/C joint tear. Puncture wounds. Traumatic brain damage. General appearance of somebody that had mistaken a giant cheese grater for a Slip 'N Slide. Medical staff assumed I had a speech impediment until my wife made them look in my mouth, where they noticed that I'd bitten through my tongue so hard that it hinged in half and teeth chipped. Francesca kept our two boys away from the hospital, but when I finally came home through the front door in a brain-damaged daze, taking small, shuffling steps, in a titanium back brace, leaning on a walker, they said my face looked like Frankenstein.

Brain damage is a trip. You can feel parts not working. I'd look at words, aware that I knew how to read, yet they'd appear like Japanese characters, which I do not know how to read. Thoughts that had zipped and connected with other thoughts within microseconds were reduced to hobbled singularity, staggering across the horizon line of my mind, so weak that I could watch as they slowed before collapsing from exhaustion.

It is very confusing getting hit by a truck.

Not at all what I had imagined.

One time I was lying on the sofa covered in sheets to absorb the blood that still leaked from the road rash weeks after impact, my damaged nervous system locking me into seized spasms, frozen and tense, consciousness slowly being untethered. It felt like the Velcro of body and awareness, which had always felt hooked and intertwined as one, had been pulled apart. Disconnected, I was still able to hear one of my friends, watching my body seize, say, "This is so unfair."

Then, like a missile fired from somewhere distant, hidden behind the chaotic storm of pain, disorientation, and anxiety within me, a clear response shot out, so unwavering in trajectory that it cut through all disorder frictionless without losing velocity.

How can they get it so wrong?

I came out ahead.

I'd do it all again to get to this point.

WTF?

Where did that come from?

Broken brain or not, I knew enough to know that those thoughts were not how one is supposed to think about getting hit by a truck. They arrived with total conviction, as if all debates were long settled and rules of logic established eons ago. **I was presented with invincible gratitude, a complete understanding that I had yet to comprehend, sealed in a black box somehow smuggled back while everything else was crashing and burning.**

But then my wife went for a beach run two weeks later and came back excitedly showing me her phone. "Look! You can still see all the blood and police markings!" Bright orange spray paint marked evidence, including the blood that had pumped out of my head and run into the gutter. Whatever—there was no connection. Not on the surface at least, but that night I had my first-ever panic attack.

Oh, remember how I just beat my chest about the joys of being uncertain, the educational, disorientated flailing in the kook zone? Time to call me on my bullshit—I did *not* want to be this deep into the unknown. I had never felt this lost in my life.

TONY HAWK "Francesca called, and she wasn't being evasive, but definitely not giving me the gravity of the whole thing. It all happened so fast and was such an emergency situation. My wife, Cathy, and I were home and I just took off and went straight to the hospital, thinking more that you were just there to be checked out. That was the vibe I got—just to monitor or check up. And then I got there and your entire face was covered in blood and you clearly had no idea what was happening. I knew that there were other injuries, but it was so clear that you had a traumatic brain injury and that your head had been bleeding. A lot. It kind of freaked me out that you had been there for a while and they hadn't cleaned the blood all over your face. That's when I was like, 'Holy shit, this is the worst accident I've ever seen.' Right when I saw you, I texted Cathy: This is really bad."

As my brain and body slowly began to heal over the months and my calendar filled with doctor, physical therapist, surgeon, psychologist, and chronic pain specialist appointments, it became evident that my chosen misfit activity might have saved my life. **I always imagined scenes where a befuddled doctor says, "You don't understand—you should be dead" or "I'm still trying to figure out how you survived" as being cool. But when you feel destroyed, it is not cool at all.** It is, in fact, the last thing Humpty wants to hear from people in charge of putting you back together again.

It does make you curious about how you did survive, though. For any seasoned skater, a sizable part of our lives has been concentrated on getting ourselves into the safest crash position. It enters the realm of an art form. Every serious skater has had to untangle feet at twenty mph, adjust impact positioning mid-descent to land on the meatiest and least bony part of the body, tighten the neck to avoid snapback concussions. Veteran skaters have adjusted for crash position hundreds of thousands of times, and that repetition fine-tunes reaction time.

Left with nothing but damage, I reverse-engineered my injuries. My left knuckles were ripped open and the tendons damaged. I hypothesized that as I was flipping over the truck and my skateboard helmet was flying off, I instinctively put my hand on my head to absorb some impact.

Centrifugal force still wound up and whipped my head to the pavement, but my forehead had no rips above the eyebrow, so I'm assuming my hand was there. My nose was ripped open and reduced to rubble as it smashed through my skull. I figured my left hand, along with biting my tongue, helped absorb some of the brain-damaging impact. It makes sense that I scorpioned, the type of slam where you land on your chest and head area and your legs whip up over your head, hard enough to explain the break in my spine. My bike had been bent into some kind of angry origami and came to rest almost a block away, a trail of its broken parts leading back to where my body stopped. I'm assuming I skipped and skidded for a bit, considering the road rash that ripped skin off.

With the mystery of how I survived kinda solved, I proceeded to deal with injuries. I was messed up, but I'd gone into anaphylactic shock seven times before, broken fingers, a rib, an arm and a leg, snapped ligaments and torn meniscuses, busted my nose and KO'd myself a couple times, even had my tongue stitched up before. This accident was simply a grab bag of injuries, but same diff, right? I know how to deal with injuries.

Wrong.

I was fucked. The whole was so much greater than the parts. Emotions hadn't been attached to injuries since I was a child, but now—with brain broken, diagnosed with PTSD, nervous system damaged and re-coding itself to survive future truck hits—my feelings had gone septic and were leaking into deep cracks that I never even knew I had in me.

I'd never thought of suicide before, but there was a moment in the

hospital when I awoke with no situational awareness because of brain damage. I was lying on some sort of body tray, my head, body, and arms tightly strapped down. Unable to focus my eyesight, I tried to find clues as to what was happening and flicked my fingers, which hit a wall, and I realized that I was sealed in a container so tight that only inches separated it from my restrained body. I understood that the inability to visually focus was due to the smooth roof of the container being inches away, which was the *last* thing I wanted to understand. I had no idea of how I got there and what was happening. It was like awakening into a nightmare where you find yourself buried alive in a coffin.

My only thought was escape as sheets of sweat soaked me, but I could feel my brain not working right. As I shook uncontrollably against the restraints, emotional and spiritual fire alarms and air raid sirens began howling inside my head. Emotions felt like hurricane winds tearing themselves apart.

I'm optimistic and always think there's a way out, a solution, but I felt there was no way to escape, no option, no sense of choice, a total absence of control unlike anything I had ever felt before. I'd never experienced being so alone, so powerless, so totally without agency in my life, and I felt myself crack in a way that I knew I would never fully recover from.

And then, without warning, an answer arrived with supernatural warmth and comfort: I will kill myself. It was like being naked on an ice floe lost in an Arctic sea, hostile frozen winds whipping, ice blistering skin on contact, and then that answer arriving like a fluffy blanket fresh from the dryer to swaddle me in supernatural warmth.

I would escape by killing myself. That would take me away from the pain, eject me into something else. Hahaha! I figured out how to give myself a choice, to give myself a sense of control. There was no debate. No weighing pluses and minuses. No thoughts of loved ones. I may have physically been in a La Jolla hospital, lying in a full-body MRI machine, within inches of the smooth inside of a tube for better imaging, strapped down to protect my injured spine and neck . . . but I existed alone at that moment.

If I'd had a gun, I would have put it into my mouth like a baby with a pacifier. I say this with a total lack of frivolity. It is not meant to be a cute sentence. I grew up knowing my dad had tried to kill himself by shooting himself in the head when he was a teenager. He'd survived and gotten the help he needed, as well as a glass eye. But I feel the need to be honest about how surprisingly comforting the decision would have been at that moment.

My "solution" relaxed me enough for me to pass out, but the event seared itself into my brain, the only vivid memory of my time in the hospital.

Now, weeks later and couch-trapped, I didn't know what to do with *that* experience. I know what it's like to fully commit—no, to fully *embrace*—the idea of suicide as a viable solution. That has a way of shattering any sense of who you think you are, even if you never feel that way again.

I was quickly put on a conveyor belt moving through the medical-industrial complex. Most attending medical professionals stated a goal of getting me as close as possible to where I was pre-accident, but that seemed like defining a life by what was taken away, a life cursed with a subtraction sign.

I went to appointment after appointment for six months while doctors and specialists did what they did—checking impersonal boxes, moving me to the next step, next doctor, next treatment down the line. Some things fully healed and some went sideways. My sympathetic nervous system was so damaged that physical contact often made me feel like I

was being electrocuted. I walked hunched over to my side, unable to find my center line, twitched uncontrollably, was unable to sequence memories, had a low stimulation threshold, was mired in coagulated depression and energy-sucking anxiety.

Regardless of the glaringly obvious unfinished business, the medical establishment checked the last box and dismissed me with congratulatory tones, considering I should be dead and all. (Not all doctors—my GP Dr. Rathbun, a neurologist named Dr. Blumenfeld, and Septembre Flannery, a dedicated private physical therapist who spent years implementing solutions, were amazing.)

Almost all the doctors reiterated, naturally, that I should never skateboard again.

I hadn't realized that I had been stuck in a broken loop, feeling like a victim with zero agency as I passively waited for the medical establishment to fix me, and now I was definitely un-fixed yet the system had dismissed me. It took an embarrassingly long time, and then only when I was kicked to the curb, for me to realize I was conforming to a system that clearly wasn't working for me.

"It was pretty clear that your head injury was taking its toll," Tony says. "It wasn't something to compare to what we all knew from getting knocked out, and it was going to take more than just some cookie-cutter therapy. You had no sense of time. Things that had happened to us weeks and years prior were all in the same time frame for you."

I'd never blindly skipped down the conventional pathway so eagerly. It *really* clicked when an Ivy League–educated neurologist (not Dr. Blumenfeld) threw up his hands and said he didn't really know how my brain would heal or exactly what to expect, and dismissed me from our last appointment by handing me a paper, radically degraded from too many generations of photocopying, displaying information on traumatic brain injury support groups.

That dude hadn't ever smashed his head. He didn't know what it *felt* like inside a TBI—a traumatic brain injury—only what he learned at a sterile academic distance. I needed somebody with experience who shared an unconventional approach to injury and recovery.

Ed had broken two vertebrae in his neck and was recovering from a most gruesome leg break. He has the rare ability to distill wisdom from approaching life with absolutely no preconceived sense of how it "should" be. I needed an Ed infusion, so I filled an email with questions and shot up a flare. His response was like me having an oxygen mask placed over my face, unaware of how long it had been since I had been able to take a long, deep, clarifying breath.

ED TEMPLETON EMAIL: *I think the truth is things just happen. Any other circumstance and you could have died, but you didn't. And that's what's amazing, that we can even think that thought. If a cat survives getting hit by a car he's not thinking about what could have happened, he's just living. But we have that ability to wonder. Same for my leg, I was thinking about all the things I could have done differently. I felt weird, but did not listen to my body. I'm old, I don't skate enough. So many factors. Did it jumping out of a trick I have done a billion times. It was time to pay the piper. No rhyme or reason. Everything aligned to cause the break, ruin our trip to Europe, and keep me laid up for a month and crippled for who knows how long.*

I'm glad you are alive. You are a resilient human to come out of that.

Best,
ed

Finally, momentum! Connection! Ed had stripped the victim varnish off with his unique blend of humor and dry absurdist wisdom. *I'm just a cat that got tagged by a truck by the beach!* For the first time since getting hit by a truck I felt some sense of direction. Gone was the feeling of being peer-pressured, even with the best intentions, to perceive my accident a certain way.

Removing myself as the victim was necessary to move into a different recovery direction, but I still didn't know what to do with this trippy, overwhelming sense of gratitude for the accident that I possessed. Since the accident I had noticed an inability to cleanly distinguish between good and bad, as if they existed in sterile vacuums that prohibited contact and any sort of blending. People kept saying this accident was a "bad" thing, but something inside of me furiously disagreed.

I'm telling you, when you get hit by a truck shit gets weird. Some part of me was processing this whole experience on another level, a level that continually kicked me into the cosmic kook zone.

My body, brain, and mental well-being were all suffering, but that annoying sparkly sense of gratitude haunted everything on an ethereal level that continually confused any conceptualization of the truck's hitting me. As my brain slowly repaired and my thinking improved, there was a memory found that did not act like any other memory. Incredibly vivid, outside of any sense of time or place, it was as if everything had been atomized and flowing, a connective awareness unlike anything I've experienced "here." There was no sense of separation. The idea of "me" as an isolated entity was so wildly ludicrous that it didn't even merit thought. There was no fixed identity locked and moving through time, no before and after, no boundaries, no grasping at anything.

It was/is the best.

Somehow it made me unable to believe what a bargain I got out of the whole deal . . . except I had no understanding of what that even meant. The last thing I wanted to do was *think* this, and the damn thing got around that by arriving as a complete experience.

Imagine telling people—when you struggle with brain damage and PTSD, need a walker, have a face laced with stitches and a pre-reconstruction nose being held in place by a plastic cast—that getting hit by a truck is one of the best things that can happen to you.

It does not go over well.

Trust me.

I needed help, very unconventional help. Mentally reviewing my friends' damage reports, I remembered Mat Hoffman, the BMX legend who has had over fifty surgeries, concussed himself double-digit times, was hit by a semitruck. The guy had even flatlined twice. I filled an email with questions, detailed my experience and subsequent struggles, and fired it off to Mat. (Multiple communications have been edited together for space and clarity.)

> **MAT HOFFMAN EMAIL:** *Hey Sean. Yeah, for the first couple months I would always drift into la-la land and space out often, but it would usually lessen after the first two months. As far as solitude, experiences like this do change your life. I used to joke that I'm living on extra credit, so if I die tomorrow I'm lucky I got this far. For me it's a dark peace. This doesn't make sense to anyone, so I stopped saying it. You looked death in the eye and took your life back. Not many people have this experience. It's a small club. When you've lived through the worst then things don't get to you the same way. I don't feel it's a brain damage thing. It's a psychological thing.*
>
> *My pain threshold has sort of evolved in the same way. If I got a compound fracture tomorrow it wouldn't hurt as much now cause I've seen this before and worse and I've recovered, so*

*the psychological pain doesn't exist, which is the most powerful
pain that endorphins can't numb. When you have control over
your mind your body naturally goes into shock and can numb
the physical pain through your endorphins giving you more control over pain and therefore less fear of risk.*

*When you have an idea of what death is like and need to
identify with someone it's near impossible. When you can't talk to
people about this isolated feeling a near-death experience gives
you it just makes you feel more isolated. Even if your friends and
family sincerely want to help, it's so taboo they trip out and can't.
I now understand that if you haven't experienced this you can't
identify.*

*Sequencing for me is more under control now but I know
what you're talking about. This seems to hang on as you heal and
gets better over time, but that can take up to seven years. I think
you'll always have a little of this but it's not the time vertigo like
it may feel like now. The isolation, pain, sweating is all part of
the post-traumatic stress but it will lessen. A piece of it will always be with you, but I think you become used to it and I think
it eventually makes you stronger.*

I hope this helps.

*your friend
-Mat*

Apparently Stacy's bent antenna was picking up signals, because he
reached out to me when I needed it most. He had recently lost his son,
so my getting hit by a truck paled in comparison. His advice wasn't some
self-help cliché about lemons and lemonade—I knew that the man himself had recently walked his talk.

"Listen closely as you are healing right now," he texted after a few back-and-forths. **"When abrupt and radical things like this happen in our lives it is strangely an opening and an opportunity to see things differently.** Pay close attention to what you're feeling and thinking and good will come of it."

He offered to make himself available whenever I needed him, and I took him up on it. On one of our calls he started laughing when I did my best to explain how life now refracted off this weird atomized experience like light hitting a spinning disco ball. I was dazzled and had no idea what was happening. "I feel like I cheated because this awareness can feel so good and all I had to do was get hit by a truck."

"Enjoy this as much as possible, it's truly a once-in-a-lifetime experience," he said. "You're going to remember this time forever. I'm so stoked for you. I know it's not easy, but it's profound."

Ed, Mat, and Stacy never once used the word "bad" to describe my getting hit by a truck. None of my outcast friends said it shouldn't have happened, which helped encourage a sense of discovery rather than avoidance.

In turn, this made me question why I continually questioned what to do with the incomprehensible atomized experience. Without being aware of it, I was scrambling for an authoritative position, fighting to be in command, to have a choice. I was scared of this giant unknown, of the lack of understanding and direction, and my reaction was to find a way to control it. *That* was the problem—not the experience. The answer was that I don't have to do *anything* with it—it's already doing it. I don't have to assert ownership over it, just get out of the way, fool.

Septembre had found a technique that specifically helped damaged nervous sytems, which made all the difference, and after over a year

of intense thrice-weekly physical therapy sessions, lots and lots of talks with Stacy encouraging me to remain open to the unknown, support from family and friends, I knew it was time. My skateboard was in the garage, untouched since the truck hit me. I drove to Tony's ramp warehouse. I needed to be alone for this.

I put on a helmet, full pads and took it slow, unsure, scared of how my reaction time and balance might have eroded, all things considered. Would I tense up and tip over like most first-timers on a board? Whip out?

I put my front foot on the board and pushed ever so lightly, and as if skating were hardwired into me, my muscle memory kicked in immediately and I gently rolled across the concrete in a way that felt beautifully familiar, the most familiar of any movement in over a year.

I didn't realize how much I'd missed the simple sensation of being part of a smooth gliding motion, how therapeutic it might be. Yes, after a life mutated by a misfit passion, it took me this long to tap back into it. For whatever reason, I had to go through the misfit cycle in its entirety to find the unconventional answer.

After maybe forty-five minutes of elementary skating and confidence-building, I climbed atop a medium-sized ramp. Pushing my board over the coping, I let it balance for minutes, secured by my back foot's awaiting my front foot and the shift as my weight went over the precipice.

Once I dropped in and rode down the ramp, my brain and nervous system would have to anticipate abrupt changes of direction, gravity, velocity. Micro adjustments in balance would be demanded to stay centered over a rolling object shooting down an incline. If there was delay in muscles firing, compression, flexibility, then I would be out-of-sync, either leaning too far forward and piledriving my body into the ground (best-case slam scenario) or leaning back too far and whipping out uncontrollably, unable to get myself into a "safe" crash position, and most likely hitting my head.

THE DIZZINESS OF THE KOOK ZONE

I hit my tail, lifting the back wheels back up and over the coping toward me on the deck. I was scared. If this went wrong, I could be doing permanent damage to myself. This was a completely different level of risk vs reward than rolling across the ground.

Taking some breaths, I clicked it back over the coping and without allowing myself to think leaned forward, compressed, and rode cleanly down the ramp. There were no thoughts needed, a lifetime of fluid reactions flowed and I found myself riding up another transition instead of splayed across the floor.

Dropping in again was awesome, but it wasn't until a few weeks later that I realized I had really healed. Gradually increasing my skate time, speed, and the complexity of what I was attempting, I messed up and found myself hitting the polished cement before I could get my hands up or twist into a better position. My breath was pulled out of me as my chest took full impact, that sting of slapping concrete flushing through my right elbow and hand, that cold flash of shock squirting into my veins. It was the hardest slam I'd had since getting hit by a truck, and I waited to see if I might start seizing, pass out, maybe pee my pants.

I waited. And waited. Nothing. It just hurt. Beautiful simple pain radiated across my chest, my shoulder, out to my elbow, and it felt so great that I started laughing—slightly unhinged, I'll admit, but the joy over knowing that I could eat shit once again, take a serious slam, was the surest measurement that I had healed.

It wasn't until I slammed that I understood what recovery meant to me. It wasn't an absence of pain, it was being able to absorb a catastrophic experience and still approach life in a way that allowed me to discover, take risks, and slam without feeling like a victim.

I lay on the cold concrete floor for a while, enjoying the pain, know-

ing that I was going to get back up and try to land the trick again, and knowing that it mattered to nobody else, held no perceivable value and would make zero difference to anybody but me.

I was back.

And, with help from friends, I had learned what to do when hit by a truck.

ELEVEN

GET A JOB, YA BUM

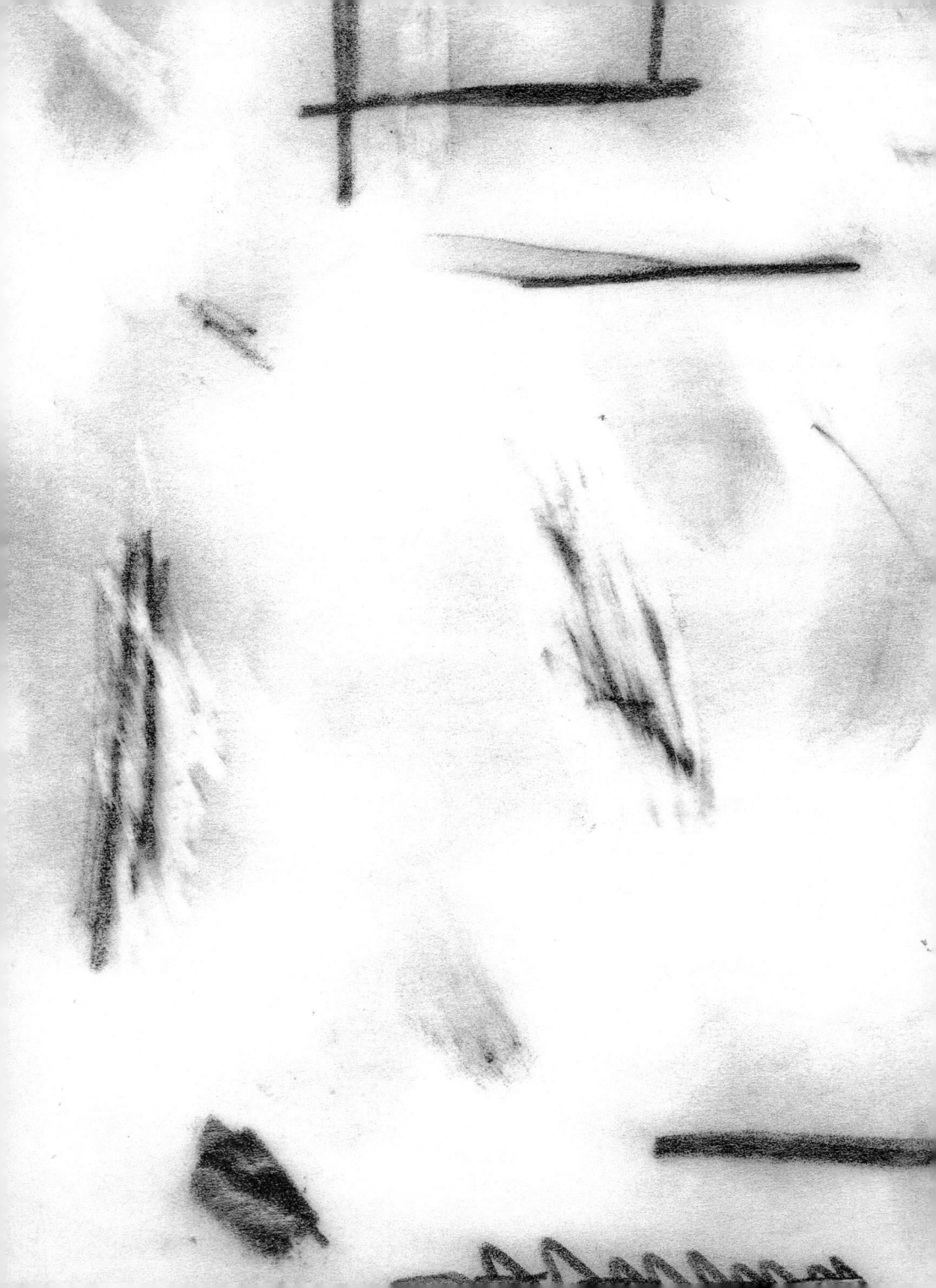

22

The Misfit Hustle

STACY PERALTA "My first real job was at eleven as a paperboy for two years and then a busboy. I was taught very early to have a job, be independent, and have my own money, so when I was seventeen and Larry Gordon came to me with a contract and said we want to sponsor you and put your name on a board and we're going to pay you fifty cents a board and if we sell twenty thousand boards a month then we'll pay you ten grand a month? You have to understand, I knew he wasn't doing this because he liked me, he was doing this because he knew I was going to sell boards for him.

"Now I'm getting paid to do a lot of illegal things like going into schools to skate the playgrounds. I have to sneak into backyard pools. Why? Well, it's part of my job. Every backyard pool I get into has the potential to get me into the magazine, which I have to do for my job, so I'm going to call photographers and take them to new pools and break the law to do it and I'm getting paid to

> do that. I realized this is a job. They're not giving me this opportunity because I'm a cool kid."

As an adult, people in positions of power no longer hold Mark down and forcibly cut his hair, but they still call him names, pointing and saying, "There goes a billion-dollar composer." As a musician scoring soundtracks for hit movies like *Thor: Ragnarok, The Life Aquatic, The Lego Movie*, and *A Minecraft Movie,* he's set unexpected tunes to films that have combined for over a billion bucks at the box office, warranting the "name-calling." Then there are his compositions providing soundtracks to various stages of life for multiple generations, with TV shows like *Pee-wee's Playhouse, Rugrats, Beakman's World, What We Do in the Shadows, Regular Show* and video games like *Crash Bandicoot* and *Ratchet & Clank: Rift Apart.*

If you visit Mark at his place of work, you will not get very far in a straight line. You may even walk in circles. Mutato Muzika is exactly the business building one would expect Mark to own, a bright green circular structure sitting like a precariously landed flying saucer in the middle of Hollywood.

The interior of Mutato Muzika—exactly the business name one would expect Mark to pick—makes an equally strong impression. It took a few trips to the bathroom before I noticed that this is where Mark stores his numerous awards. While we walked down curved hallways searching for a suitable space to talk, show business buzzed by outside on Sunset Boulevard, reflected back onto itself by Mutato's mirrored windows.

The entertainment industry, show business, isn't bashful about its intent—just check out the name. It is an industry using entertainment to

make money. This requires highly creative people like Mark to work with highly uncreative people in order to have a career in the biz. When studios and streaming services are run by lawyers with armies of accountants beholden to shareholders who value profit above all else, even being a billion-dollar baby cuts little slack. In order to keep doing what he loves, Mark has never stopped mutating (Mutatoing?) from a legally blind kid to bespectacled outcast booby-trapping music with subversive wisdom to a favorite composer for directors allergic to conventional soundtracks.

For misfits moving along their path, there comes a time when life's responsibilities increase, which often requires an uptick in interactions with the mainstream in one way or another. This is the part of the misfit journey that requires perhaps the most conscious assessments and planning, because now you must strategize how to work within a system that isn't designed for your irregular edges. You have an appreciation of your value in misfit currency, but now that has to be exchanged for mainstream legal tender.

Luckily, there are a few options for the misfit. **You can go the hermit route, basically quit society and find a nice metaphorical isolated cave.** My friend lives in a four-hundred-square-foot 1940s-era bungalow. He requires very little to survive. Every time I visit the only entertainment detectable is art, objects demonstrating misfit passion, and an old orbital plastic radio droning in the background.

Other outcasts change the world so that a rejected misfit passion kicks its way into the mainstream with its own industry. Tony and Stacy fought to prevent skateboarding from going the way of the Hula-Hoop, and now people ride toys in the Olympics. Shepard's OBEY and Roger's Beyond the Streets transformed a social blight into appreciated art that provides livelihoods for "criminals." Dr. Jon's board game shop trans-

formed what was considered harmful escapism into appreciated education.

This necessary interaction requires constant tinkering to integrate meeting increasing responsibilities with staying true to our misfit selves. Naturally, the status quo guardians have established guardrails to keep us all in line. In many cultures a job defines you socially, but veteran misfits are beyond stale conventional classifications.

Let's use an "extreme" example to show how fluid and pointless a job title is to your life. I've been friends with Tony through multiple peaks and valleys in skateboarding popularity. I've seen him struggle financially and be rudely dismissed by potential employers, openly laughed at over his "career" as a seemingly failed pro skater in the 1990s. Then I've seen him internationally celebrated and financially rewarded as the face of alternative sports a decade later—suddenly he had a "dream job" that parents fantasized about their kids having. Absolutely *nothing* changed regarding Tony's perspective and work ethic.

By now you know the worth of being a misfit and understand what's at stake if you lose that essence. It helps to understand that there are ways to work in the mainstream system without getting lost within it. **Some occupations in the arts require creativity, and eccentrics are able to modulate their unique POVs to sneak their sparkly strangeness into straight society.** Perhaps you can compartmentalize and hold your creativity as if it were breath and exhale when you have your own space. Every misfit I know has, in one way or another, had to grind it out at various points in imaginatively barren jobs.

But motivated misfits can't help but bring innovation and energy into their projects, and this often leads to new types of jobs. When DEVO broke up, Mark mutated his musical outlook into something less overtly confrontationally questioning—there are no lyrics in his soundtrack orchestral compositions—but still recognizably "out there."

Was this a failed dream crumbling? A step backward? Listen to "Ping Island," one of his most famous compositions from a movie, and you'll be pushed into a joyful oddball space. Millions of people are still exposed to Mark's misfit communications, and he's often quoted as saying you can also "change things from the inside working out." You know, like a misfit virus. Worked for the plague.

What may at first appear as a failure—the destruction of the initial vessel of a misfit passion—may simply be misfit evolution demanding change. Mark had been mired in poverty and slept in freezing industrial spaces, dodged angry beer bottles on stage, giggled at early promoters paying DEVO to *stop* playing, but he knew that this approach was not going to last. Early on he understood the need to maneuver within a larger traditional system if he wanted an occupation making his music.

Mark has witnessed many talented misfit friends struggle due to an inability to hone a necessary adaptive technique. This is why, when Mark and I do exit the hallway loop into an open-windowed meeting room and start talking about the benefits of the misfit journey, he makes an immediate distinction. "What kind of misfits are we talking about?" He points out the window onto Sunset Boulevard. "Because there are a lot of misfits sleeping on bus benches out there."

And he's right. We all know misfits living on "Struggle Street," as Michelle puts it. DEVO went from playing sold-out stadiums to being dropped by their label—legit rock star hero to zero in a matter of years. So what makes the difference between Mark and other creative oddballs sleeping on bus benches?

"It can be tough," Mark says. "People have to figure things out. I never bought into rock star bullshit. I always felt that even when things were good for us, enjoy it now because it's going to be over soon. I *always* had that feeling. People get to that stage where they have a hit record and they don't know how to go forward or they don't know what forward is—they don't want it to change. I feel bad for them."

When DEVO fizzled, Mark began making music for commercials, and then an old friend, Paul Reubens, aka Pee-wee Herman, asked him to score his new TV show. Mark didn't exactly know how to soundtrack, but knew how to write songs so he figured he could DIY a new occupation. "I had a talent for writing music for pictures, but I didn't know that at the time," he says.

Think about this for a second—**Mark had experienced being extremely successful yet still approached life like a teenager trying to figure out what he wanted to do.** His eagerness and lack of hesitancy revealed not only a new opportunity but a new talent. While excited to work with a friend as bonkers as Reubens, Mark had no idea of the proper way to score live action. "I'd watch a piece of film and when Pee-wee came down the staircase I would make this piece of music. I would have to count it off so we could all play along to the playback."

Mark was so inexperienced and hustling so hard that he didn't realize how difficult he was making his new job. "It wasn't until the end of the season that the editor said, 'You know, Mark . . . I was wondering how come you record all the pieces separately and don't record them to SMPTE timecode? That's how you lock your music up to the film.' I looked at him: You can do that? I'd scored a whole year, thirteen episodes, before I found out about something that would have been taught in the first year at film school."

Raw. Highly motivated. Highly inexperienced. Mark's amateur energy to learn and explore new expressions while being incredibly disciplined opened another professional outlet for his creativity. He credits the unplanned hustle of scoring Pee-wee with changing the trajectory of his career. "I didn't think I was going to be a film composer, that's for sure," Mark says.

SACHA JENKINS "I benefited from having an artistic mother and an artistic father and having an understanding that culture has value, that there is commodity in culture. At a young age, I was able to connect with the understanding that writing on trains and going to hardcore shows—all these things have value. I didn't know at the time that it was necessary monetarily, I thought it was value to me, that it meant something to me. Because it means something to me—that's valuable. I wasn't thinking in terms of dollars and cents, but eventually it did turn into dollars and cents."

A lucrative professional skateboarding career may have been my dream, but it was not in the books. When that didn't happen, I had already pivoted to writing as a way to stay in the culture that I loved. With no college degree, I started writing for skate mags, where, admittedly, the bar and the pay were extremely low. But after a few articles, I had learned from my friends how to rub those small sticks together to generate some heat. I understood there were not a lot of writers that knew the alternative sports world, so I used that marginalization as something to make me stand out and get into gigs that paid more.

Sending clips to bigger mainstream magazines proved I was publishable, and editors assigned me pieces on skate culture for newspapers like the *LA Times*. I made deadlines, was courteous and creative, did everything possible to make *their* job easier. You would not believe how far not being a flake gets you in these situations, allowing you to practice with the pros, build relationships, and move on to bigger projects. When I was eventually hired as a magazine editor, paid to work on documentaries and write books, not a single person asked about college degrees.

Traditionalists often ignore how a degree no longer automatically slots you into a dream job, yet they'll still downgrade the misfit hustle spilling over into livelihoods. But a motivated misfit has what can't be taught—an unconventional way of thinking. "People that want to be a film composer, they go to a university and learn all the techniques, yet they don't teach them how to be creative," Mark says. "Instead, they become the best orchestrators. They end up working for people like me. They take my music, which was made on a couple of keyboards, and turn that into something a hundred-piece orchestra can play because that's the part they learned at school."

Motivated misfits will find ways to transcend cultural lessons and they can bring that attitude into the workplace—after all, we've trained ourselves to climb fences, metaphorical and literal. "People are afraid of what they don't know, mostly," Mark says. "What I would say to kids is that the best thing you can do if you wanted to learn is by finding a way to go watch people that are doing what you want to do. Just watch and see how they do it."

A teenager recently came to Mark's studio to fly-on-the-wall. "He probably learned more just sitting here watching me write a theme song for a TV show than he would have in a semester of film composition at school, because he's watching somebody do it in the real world," Mark says. "Sometimes, just being exposed to it is enough. Find a way to watch what they do, even if it means that you offer to run and get them food at lunchtime or clean up the studio after they're done."

Seeing the sausage being made is an easy way to remove the fear of learning something new. "For me," Mark says, "the most surprising thing was how easy it was once I started doing it."

Misfits who achieve their goals know the importance of educating

themselves through experience. And, in my experience, we want to help, so just ask somebody who has achieved a level of success in what you are interested in. "You can offer your services to people that you respect or admire, people that are doing things that you're interested in," Sacha, like Mark, advises. "Carry equipment. Offer to drive cars. Offer to help in any way you're capable of helping without the experience."

And while you are finding ways into a world that may have seemed closed off, get busy being a passionate amateur. "The other best thing is just to do it," Sacha says. "It's easier said than done, but you can make a zine—there are things you can do that are within your power, even if they're super primitive. If someone sees that you're doing something, it might inspire someone to help you or further develop what you're doing. You gotta do shit *in real life.*"

School has grading systems that conformists love binding to future success, but for misfits used to making their own way, skilled at riding obstacles, the supposed limitations of lower grades can also be a guide. "I'm very realistic about how modest my natural gifts as an artist are," Shepard says. "There are people I know who can draw like Michelangelo, they can do things very quickly, and I take some pride in that it's my work ethic and not my natural talent that gets me through. The way I deal with art is like being an athlete that is well conditioned. I am in practice making things every single day, and if there's a deadline, I'm going to meet that deadline. Some people say, 'Oh, I wasn't inspired,' but you have to reach inside and find it."

Reaching inside to "find it" is a skill that misfits must hone if they intend to persevere in unconventional careers. "I see a phenomenon with people where they develop some mastery and they think that they've reached a level where the world owes them something," Shepard says. "A lot of those people end up being bitter and their careers stall, and the reason is because confidence and some talent only goes so far—there has to be a continuous drive."

In the midst of battling the fear that you screwed your life up, how do nonconformists finding their way remain steadfast and dedicated to the misfit hustle? "When I look back on what I've been able to accomplish," Roger says, "I really look back to my teenage years, and it was as simple as if you tell someone that you're going to send them a picture, then you send them a picture. You tell someone that you're going to show up at four in the afternoon, you'd better have a really good reason if you don't."

I don't know if it's the chicken or the egg, but I've noticed that misfits who carved out unique "successful" careers thrive by being incredibly responsible while remaining open to opportunities. "Success is tied to being able to see when doors open, when they close, and how long they will be open," Sacha says. "All of these things that have happened for me happened because I saw an opportunity in the distance—I didn't know what was going to happen, but I ran toward that door."

TONY HAWK "A lot of people I know leaned into their skateboard experiences to learn new ways to make a living. If they were filming their friends skating, they learned how to film for theatrical releases because they already knew how to move with a camera and keep somebody in frame. Some top filmmakers got their start in skate videos back in the early days when nobody was paying them—look at Spike Jonze. Or maybe people start brands that were rooted in their culture or ethos. It's more about the hustle. You have to hustle to follow your passion. If you have that kind of hustle to just participate in this kind of activity, then you're definitely going to have it in droves trying to find a career. You have to hustle to make things work, and you don't lose the spirit even if things are working. If you have massive success, then you're still thinking, 'What's next, what should I be doing?'"

23

You Have a Unique Voice, So Use It

A hidden fact of misfit life is that there are always *way* more out-casts out there than you think, and the camouflaged nature of this detail means that incredibly untapped opportunities are out there waiting for the right nonconformist. Brian Flynn is a person with many fringe passions, and he takes them to such a detailed level that every conversation I've had with him leads to talk in differentials in the fractions of an inch. He can't help himself. Crazy technical misfit-nerd stuff. He knows I don't collect vintage Godzilla toys, but will still reel off the differences in color gradients on some obscure model. It was leaning into this fixation with the misfit hustle, and not any business plan, that created Brian's impressive career.

"When I first started collecting toys in '91, it was a little weird doing that at age twenty," he says. But passion overrode self-consciousness and the collection grew. He even began sharing his strange new hobby with some college classmates. "I found a couple people that were thinking the same way and next thing I knew, eight of us were collecting weird old toys."

As a punk, Brian collected low-quality, high-passion fanzines. At various stages participants of persecuted subcultures like graffiti, punk, street photography, and hip-hop filled their media void by handmaking enthusiastic and obviously amateur zines. Kids with no publishing experience wrote, took photos, cut-and-pasted photocopied content in an amateur design to make low-fi zines, which they traded around the globe. Cultural information was exchanged in a very primitive underground manner, but it was also a project to channel passions. Brian decided to make one about Japanese toys. "The difference was that I was a working graphic designer," he says. "The zine about collecting Japanese toys my friend and I came out with was called Super7."

Brian's expertise made the DIY project look legit. "To anybody else walking up and looking at it, it was a real magazine, but to me, it was just another zine." Approaching the project with this mentality, he used the budgetary formula many kids employed with their seventy-five-cent zines. "Okay, it's going to cost five thousand dollars to print five thousand copies? I need to sell twelve ads at two hundred and fifty dollars and sell four hundred copies at six bucks and I break even. No different than any punk band putting out their own record."

It was published with very low expectations. "Come on, we were *way* out in left field," Brian says. "We just started putting in shit that we liked. It was a magazine about Japanese toys—who is going to care?"

But, because it looked like a legit magazine, major periodical distributors picked it up, and it took off. "That was very surprising to me, that there was a ton more people out there interested in what we were talking about. It was authentic. It was real. We weren't trying to target a segment of the market. The first issue had an article about how to tell the differences between original Marusan Godzilla tail molds. Who cares about that? Well . . . I care about that."

With pages to fill and no editorial or art department, Brian called on his creative fringe friends. "No different than making a photocopied

zine—we included our friends who were artists. We just wrote about the things that we liked that we thought nobody else was writing about. It wasn't gigantic right away, but there was the realization that this really works and people are into it and we can make another issue and then another issue."

Brian loved how some Japanese toy magazines included a coupon that allowed readers to buy a limited recolor of a toy, and Super7 borrowed that idea all the way to working with a Japanese toy company. When some of the Super7 coupon recolors outsold the original-colored toys, well . . . "That is how we got into making toys," Brian says. "The people that ran the toy companies asked us what we wanted to make next."

Brian simply followed the instinct that had taken him this far and, as Sacha advised, he took advantage of a door opening, and Super7 toys was born. "We've definitely shaken up the toy industry by not having those preconceived notions of what and how things should be done," Brian says. "We just went, 'What do we want to make? Let's go make that.'"

So, basically Brian started a major toy company with worldwide distribution and hundreds of designs accidentally? "Yeah," Brian says. "I didn't go to school for toy design. I was a working graphic designer. I just started making stuff that I liked. Just start making stuff."

But how does Brian continue to stay hyped decades later and not fall into conventional traps as Super7 manages the increasing pressure of an expanding customer base, triple-digit employees, brick-and-mortar stores? "Everybody seems to play to the lowest common denominator—what is the thing that is going to apply to most people? That's how you end up with beige computers—what's the most least offensive milquetoast thing? If you want me to open up my wallet, I'm not opening it for milquetoast—show me something incredible. Get me excited. Make people care. That middle-of-the-road thing? Everybody can make that, so therefore there is nothing special about you. What is interesting and special about you? That's what's going to get people to buy what you're making."

In so many conventional settings, misfits are made to feel less-than because of our minority interests, but Brian knows how perceived strangeness can make the difference when connecting to a customer. "My wife was making custom pillows for a housewares line, and for the first launch she figured she needed some basics to hedge our bets. We made some with patterns and colors, but nobody needed them because *everybody* had patterns and colors. What people were interested in was the ones with the weird owl on them or the head silhouettes, because nobody had things that looked like that. You have a unique voice, so use it."

SACHA JENKINS "Recognition is great, but economics is really important. I'm not above thinking I could be making more money for what I do, but I think success is having a job that you like where you have the ultimate say-so. I'm working on projects, and these films aren't blockbusters, they aren't *Mission: Impossible*, they're documentaries that have ten-million-dollar budgets, three-million-dollar budgets. I'm working on projects that have budgets where people respect my opinion and want me to be able to be creative, so in that regard I consider it success. It's emotional success. I always need to be doing something creative to feel good, that I have purpose."

It might surprise people to realize how many of the misfits who are regarded as leaders or faces of a subculture struggle with what has indivertibly became a job. **Almost all the misfits I know are hypersensitive, that bent antenna tuned into a lifetime of picking up the signal when people reject your vibe.** When a misfit is unintentionally elevated into a leadership position, it often scrambles them up. Tony famously hated how winning more pro contests than any other skater in history created a sense of separation from his fellow skaters.

When I first started doing demonstrations, it was discombobulating having kids ask for autographs after the show. When we find comfort in community, it messes with you to be pushed outside of it. I didn't know how to deal with the emotional separation—I was just like them and related to fighting for what we all loved rather than being celebrated, which felt like a rejection of sorts, if that makes any sense. Separation, regardless of the reason, is still the same action.

At one of my first demos in a rural community, I remember freaking out and hiding under a table. A famous skateboarder once told me that "being a pro kinda thrashed me and I wished it didn't. It freaked me out. I always felt like an outsider through all the mess, even when it was going really well." A handful of pro skateboarders quit their "job," leaving hundreds of thousands of dollars on the table, because of the unwanted position the status placed on them. But we need leaders, and people's natural gifts and aggressive problem-solving abilities often inadvertently slot them into leadership roles.

Out of all the misfit leaders I know, not a single one had designs to lead. There is fight in all of them, but not much thirst for a throne. If anything, more of them initially considered themselves extremely ill-equipped for the job.

Michelle had just finished college, which provided no direction. "I didn't even want to go," she says. "I did that to impress my parents." So

Michelle graduated, got hooked on roller derby, moved to California, and executed a calculated plan to reimagine roller-skating. Like clockwork, right?

"I called my sister and I was like, 'I hate my life,'" Michelle says. "There was no reason to be unhappy. My sister asked what's good in my life? I answered, 'Roller derby.' She said, 'Okay, what can you improve with that?' I said the skates were ugly. She said, 'Who could help you change that?' I said, 'Nobody.' And she was like, '*No* . . . Who makes the roller skates ugly?' I said, 'The manufacturers.' She said, 'That's who you need to work with. Write to all the manufacturers, Michelle. You have nothing to lose. Otherwise, what, you're going to sit with kill-yourself vibes?'"

Michelle sent a letter with suggestions to the eight major roller skate manufacturers. Only one responded, but that was all she needed. Riedell was impressed with Michelle's passion and equally unimpressed with her inexperience. They started her with product testing and then offered her a vendor relationship with no terms—zero up-front money, but plenty of debt if the skates didn't sell. "They told me that if I sold enough of certain skates to justify making the changes then they would make a brand with me." And how does a misfit leader respond? "I didn't want to be a business owner at all!" Michelle says. "I did not trust myself."

She hedged her bets by opening a shop in the back of a children's clothing store, which occasionally doubled as her apartment. "It never felt like a good business decision, because I was always in debt—like six-digit debt sometimes," Michelle says. It was her UPS driver who recognized the word for her approach to adventure: moxie.

Subculture shops like Moxi and The Brooklyn Strategist become de facto clubhouses, especially vital at the start of new scenes, the owners and employees often becoming leaders of the community in a variety of ways. "There's a really wide range of people, ethnicities, gender identities,

social interests that come to our store," Dr. Jon says of his board game store. "How many people in the total population really enjoy building models, painting them, and getting into these very detailed battle skirmishes using measuring tape and rolling dice? The answer is probably a very small percentage of the population, yet it is a very large percentage of the diversity within that population that we see coming through our doors."

Both Dr. Jon and Michelle recognized the need to create a different experience that encourages people to not just enter the store but to dive into the subculture. Dr. Jon seems slightly less eager to jump headfirst into a mess than Michelle, but he was equally original and bold with his problem-solving. "I was doing quite a bit of research to find out what game stores were like in the country, and I realized what I was trying to bring to the table wasn't being done."

Dr. Jon talked to various board game shop owners to understand what already existed. "They'd ask how I was going to differentiate myself from all the failing game stores." Using his research background and knowledge of how the brain develops, he began gathering data and building the concept of a different type of cultural hub.

Creating a safe space for misfits is not a new idea, but Dr. Jon envisioned an educational and empowerment-charged atmosphere filling an imaginative space. Kids get to geek out in the best way possible, socialize, and express themselves while parents and participants alike are guided in reconceptualizing a fringe passion as forceful real-world empowerment.

"What differentiates our enrichment programs from just sitting and playing games is that we focus quite heavily on methods of approach for problem-solving, with all ideas being valuable—some definitely being better than others, but really working with kids to find ways to solve the dynamic problem that's in front of them. And, because the games are dynamic, it's not the same answer every time—there is no dominant strategy. You have to pivot based on what other people around you are doing."

Facing the same problem as Dr. Jon, Michelle realized she had to find creative ways to draw people in to show them the awesomeness of roller-skating subculture. But how does one advertise when there are no endemic magazines or media because there is essentially no industry? Michelle wasn't just trying to solve how to sell roller skates, she was figuring out how to sell a product that still needed to be defined. In order to do that she needed to build a culture around roller skates, which is why she started free lessons at the beach.

Essentially throwing tent revivals by the beach with an offset evangelical zeal, Michelle expanded from simple instructional sessions to wilder events encouraging self-expression. "I'd organize critical-mass-type street skates that would meet with a theme like Girl Scouts where everybody would dress up in camping gear and skate around town with lights."

Michelle showed Riedell that there was a market within the new expressive culture of roller-skating by helping create it. Finally, she had creative input, and the stale boots that had been the standard since the 1940s were redesigned and hit with a wild new color palette utilizing new materials and wrapping them with wild designs like cheetah prints and rainbows under the Moxi label.

Despite her initial success, Michelle still needed to grow the scene beyond her grassroots effort, get the funky new things in front of more eyeballs. What type of stores do young people cruise for upcoming trends? A store like Urban Outfitters has reach all over the country. Thinking like a world-builder, Michelle DIY'd a pamphlet explaining how roller-skating was a perfect fit with their vibe and went to the Urban Outfitters corporate office to talk to the buyers.

Or not. It wasn't until the cold rebuff from the receptionist, an outright refusal to even contact a low-level assistant to field her inquiry, that Michelle realized this was not how the "real" world worked. The traditional system regularly constructs barriers to keep alternative invaders like her out. But misfit leaders know how to climb traditional fences—although, in this case, it was more of a desk she had to get over.

Urban Outfitters had a lounge to the side of reception, so Michelle bought a coffee and waited for the guard to leave her tower. When the receptionist finally did get up from her chair to go around the corner, Michelle was ready with flyers in hand and ran behind the desk stuffing Moxi propaganda in company pigeonholes so that every senior member of Urban Outfitters would be exposed to the world of Moxi. Talk about taking a brand name to heart.

And when Michelle did get a call from the company letting her know it was interested in selling Moxi roller skates? "I haven't yelled like I did when Urban Outfitters called me since."

With no designs to lead, Michelle continued attacking problems that prevented growth in her subculture with the same hustle, by organizing a contest circuit, arranging international tours, and helping start a magazine. All of this put her into a leadership role, which was not always rewarding. "I always get so much shit! Whenever I'm solving a problem, it's always against the grain and there is always a ton of resistance. I could give a fuck, because my results have proven that my intentions are for this community to expand and be good for skaters."

Like Shepard and Tony, when a misfit front-runner starts earning some success, the accusation of doing it for themselves over the interests of the culture is predictably leveled. "I think that a lot of people trust me, but the ones that don't know my history or experience are the loudest ones, because it's not the way they would have done it," Michelle says. "But I can give a fuck. They're not experienced. They've never been in my

GET A JOB, YA BUM

shoes. If they had an idea that was so genius, then why aren't they out here doing it?"

A major reason that most people don't lead or world-build is this intense pressure. "Of course," Shepard says, "the internet tells me on a daily basis how much I suck." Social media's dehumanizing distance mixed with its ability to squarely land a punch makes it easy to tell each other how much we suck, but it also allows people to throw thanks. Along with her formidable physical talent, appreciation for Michelle's role is one of the reasons why so many in the community began calling her Queen, a label that isn't exactly a comfortable fit. "I don't want to be the queen," she says. "I want to be the queen *maker*. I want to make tons of queens."

Spoken like a true sprinkler of moxie dust. "I want everybody to feel exactly like I do when people compliment me."

TWELVE

THE GOLDEN AGE
OF THE MISFIT

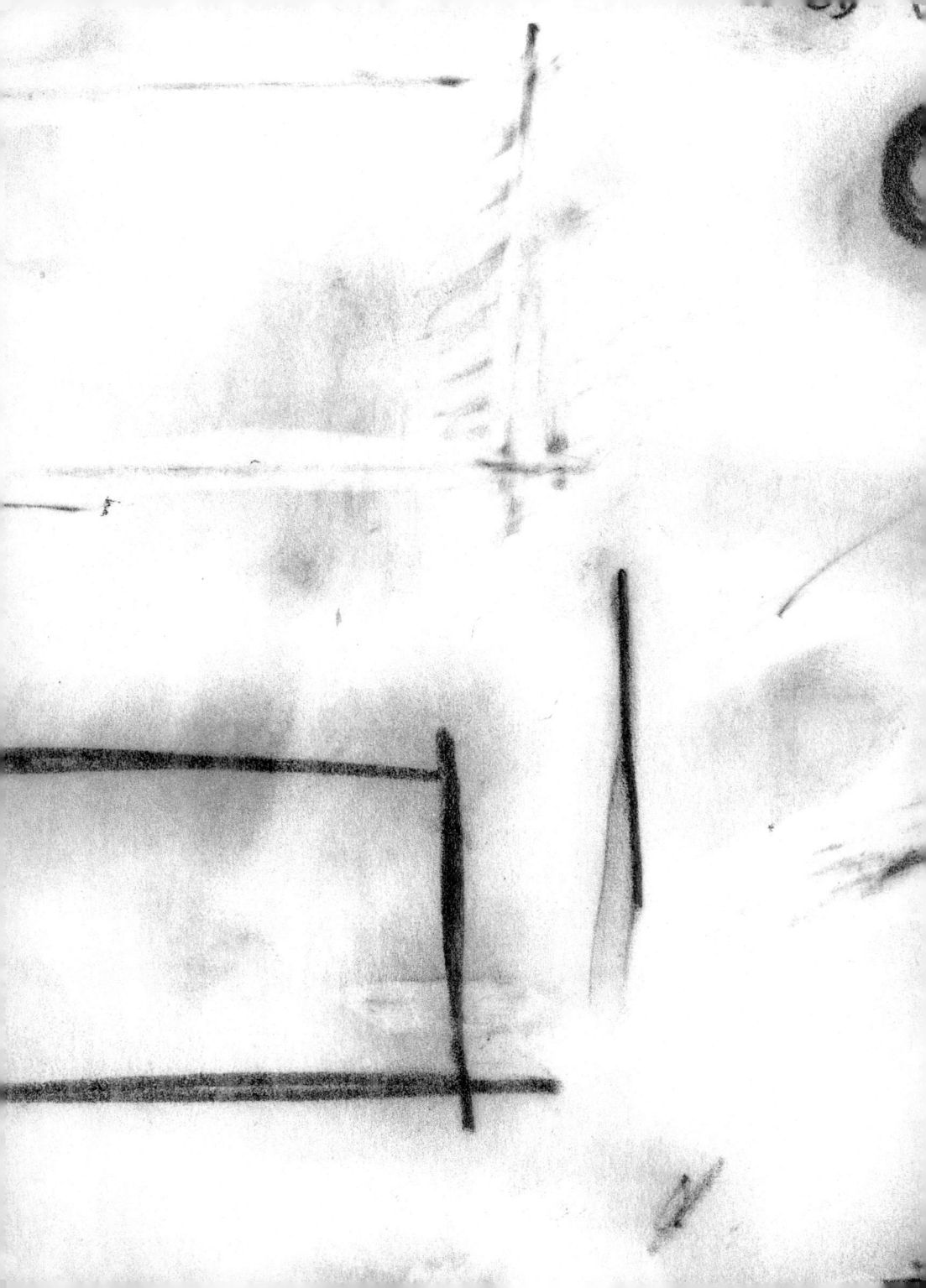

24

Jell-O Avoiding the Mold

STACY PERALTA "I was at an airport and two men stopped me and said, 'A friend of ours died and we're on our way to his funeral. It's amazing that we get to meet you here and share this because we're going to play [the 1987 skateboard video that Stacy directed] *The Search for Animal Chin* at his memorial for the entire service. It's what he would have wanted.'

"There was no processing—it bypassed my brain and went right to my emotions and heart. These guys were adults with lives and kids and families, and their friend dies and they want something from their experiences that was a touchstone. By watching *Chin* together they can have this touchstone experience again there with him.

"It meant so much to me that I reached out to Tony to tell him this, because as one of the featured skaters, he hears *Chin* stories all the time, but not like this. And I don't think *Chin* is a good film. I pretty much think it's a terrible film that I made and as a result, I never expected it to stick. You never know if what you do is going to land, and to know how many people over time it did land with is super gratifying. I knew it had reach, but I'd never have thought that it would be a unifying factor at somebody's funeral."

We all want to be successful in life but the problem for us oddballs is what exactly do we mean by that? "Success," as any misfit knows, is another one of those words that the general public assumes has a collective fixed meaning, emitting the aura of yet another elemental truth like "normal." In school when people elected the student "Most Likely to Succeed," they seemed to understand what they were voting for, whereas I never looked at the people who "won" as leading any sort of life to pine after. They weren't voting for "Most Likely to Laugh and Go Their Own Way" or "Most Likely to Harbor Lifelong Curiosity" or "Most Likely to Create Their Own Version of Victory."

The misfit issue with a word as powerful as "success" seems to be that the communal representation of the ideal says more about conformity than anything else—none of the celebrated misfits I know were ever voted to amount to anything in high school, so why expect divergent definitions to somehow align later in life?

The point of promoting the notion that one success fits all, from an outside vantage point, is to make as many people as possible chase the same carrot without asking if it's a carrot we really want. Groupthink ideals like "success" seem structured to shame people into not questioning— "D'oh, you don't know what success is?"—the erecting of a socially celebrated electric fence to keep people away from close examination. But by now we know how misfits react to fences.

Tony has seen how dedicated veteran misfits react to life and can ID it instantly, "because they have an astute sense of the world so they approach it with confidence but in a very nontraditional way," Tony says. "They know that your life doesn't have to be cookie cutter."

As a confused kid, I was constantly looking for clues on how this place worked, and from that questioning distance it was perplexingly obvious that society's version of success was not the advertised elixir it purported to be. Rich, famous, powerful people were often visibly miserable, with some quitting altogether in one way or another. "Plenty of people make a shitload of money," Tony agrees, "but their Ferrari did not bring them peace."

Let's use a symbol of success to bring some clarity to this somewhat abstract point. For the general public, the trophy is a physical representation of success, a status symbol that quickly signals who is a winner. Traditional champion athletes have trophy rooms. There are trophy wives and trophy husbands. Overpriced, overperforming cars like Ferraris can be considered wheeled trophies. Hypebeast shoes or clothes from limited drops are totable trophies. Famous winners have photos taken as they hoist or cuddle and cry over their trophies.

Consider what Tony, arguably the greatest alternative sports champion in history, did with his trophies. "I'd usually give them to kids after the contests," he told me. "I didn't want to rest on my previous accolades. I always looked to the future instead of reminiscing about past performances."

He discarded what society tells us to aim for, repurposing the brass ring from something to possess into a marker that helped him reach beyond. A trophy, even the biggest trophy in Tony's misfit world, was disconnected from his version of success. "For me it wasn't about 'the winning,'" Tony told me, "it was more about outdoing myself, skating the best I could, and trying to set new standards."

Regardless of how the amateurism embarrasses Stacy, it's telling that in *The Search for Animal Chin*, probably the most popular skateboard video in history, Tony and a gang of the world's best skaters start by looking for a prize and eventually realize that what they won was the search itself. "I think we should keep looking for Chin for the next two years," one of them reflects. "Two years?" another one immediately questions before another skater finishes the sentiment, "Next . . . rest of our life."

I like to think that at Misfit High School we'd vote on "Most Likely to Go on the Search."

SHEPARD FAIREY "A lot of people's metric for success is completely different than mine. It can be what car they're driving or what clothes they're wearing—for me all that kind of stuff did not matter at all. Luckily, when you come from middle-class white privilege and a preppy background and you embrace punk rock and skateboarding, distancing yourself from affluence is part of being cool, so then I could take being poor as an intentional thing. I could position it that way even though I was highly insecure about my lack of financial success for a long time.

"You have to be self-defined and self-determined. If your version of success is going to be dictated by someone else then you're going to be screwed, because that is always going to be a moving target. Society is fickle. Culture is fickle. If you're a creative person, then the main thing is making something that stands out from what everyone else is making. That is something that can be done with very primitive tools or sophisticated tools. There is no one way to do it. A lot of people I admire work smarter, not harder, whether it's [rapper] M.I.A. making her first record in her bedroom with very simple sampling. Everyone has to figure out what is the right path for them, what fulfills their vision.

"When I made enough money to pay for my first big run of offset prints of OBEY and [André] the Giant and I made five thousand of each print? I had a shed that was filled floor to ceiling with prints, and I looked at it and thought, *Every one of them is going to be on a street corner eventually.* To me, that was the Lamborghini in the garage."

One thing I've found through a lifetime of misfit mixing is that unconventional success is not a fixed definition, it's Jell-O avoiding the mold. Largely rejecting standardized and certified tokens of accomplishment, outsiders often seem to partially define their success through individual expression. To show you what I mean, let's examine how some successful misfits design their surroundings.

Housed within an underwhelming brick building, Shepard's work area has a distinct teenage-room vibe to it. It's as if a motivating factor in Shepard's version of success is never again having Mom tell you to clean your room. Everything about it explodes chaotic punk expression. Offset prints are stacked in various piles under desks, piles of curly discarded stencil excess sit atop cut-outs. Boxes are shoved in various areas, often adorned with random graffiti tags, as if anything remaining still for too long became vulnerable to the laws of street art. A stray Zeppelin album case (that Shepard designed) lies askew among piles of printouts and cheap newsprint zines. Computers with oversized displays glow on desks, with brainstorm debris in messy paper mounds beside keyboards. Walls are covered with friends' art in the same chaotic way that teenagers decorate. There are frames on most of them, but some are just ripped cardboard boxes or New York Transit signs.

The fact that Banksy apparently stenciled on the boxes with intriguing "Fragile" stickers is not highlighted, nor is the fact that Keith Haring vandalized the subway sign that somebody else "borrowed." They are presented with all the pomp of a stoner friend's doodles ripped out of a high school notebook and pinned up. The boxes aren't even neatly cut with a straight-edge, just torn roughly. The tape gun and empty soda bottle obscure some versions of the famous President Obama "HOPE" portrait. If you aren't down with the icky art-as-investment scene, then you wouldn't assume that the various scraps crowding the signed DEVO album would easily climb into the six figures under the auction hammer.

When Tony made his first crazy money, he searched for a very specific warehouse to locate Tony Hawk Incorporated. This quest dragged on, because the warehouse required a taller-than-normal ceiling height and a very specific structural support beam pattern to allow for the heart of the whole endeavor—a modular thirteen-foot-tall half-pipe that cost a cool million. You cannot take too many steps in any of Tony's spaces without being aware of how obsessed he is with skating. His home bathroom has a custom sink that resembles a favorite old skatepark. He poured an actual concrete skatepark in his backyard. Skateboards litter the entrance and driveway.

Michelle did him one better and bought a rural house that has ramps built into the architecture. Other ramps of various sizes pepper the property along with farm animals, so that wildlife runs around as people throw backflips out of half-pipes within spitting distance of her kitchen.

Roger lives in Los Angeles, and while the front of his home is in attractive Mission style, the back looks like a vandalized train yard, fences and guesthouse covered in graffiti done by some of the most legendary aerosol artists in the world. Some people collect Fabergé eggs, but Roger collects rusted vintage spray-paint cans that he displays by the front door. His office showcases a punk zine collection, some Sid Vicious paraphernalia, piles of sketches from people like Matt Groening and infamous NYC taggers.

Speaking of displaying objects and images that spark you, you won't find any glory shots of Tony skateboarding hanging on his home walls, but he does have a Clash tour poster and a Lebowski award plaque that was used in the film. A broken chunk of concrete embedded with orange and blue tiles, a piece of the beloved but demolished skatepark of his youth, is displayed like a gilded artifact from King Tut's tomb.

I've never seen any gold records flexing in Mark's home either, but his bathroom has a cool metallic photo of David Bowie shushing you as you pee, and somehow he got ahold of a full-sized plastic Ronald McDonald, and the clown is seated, arm stretched out as if locked in some existential limbo awaiting company as he stares out over Hollywood. Many of Mark's neighbors have golden Oscar, Emmy, and Grammy trophies, but he is visibly much more excited about a plastic clown.

But success with misfits shines in all aspects of life, not only the outward-facing. I ask Stacy how being a misfit shaped his life, and he laughed at me. "Oh, man, that's like saying what's it like having lungs and breathing? I don't know anything else. I'm in my sixties and I'm learning one of the most difficult sports I've ever learned in my entire life and I'm still going to be doing it for years to come. And I'm looking out the window right now and seeing wind, so I'm probably going to be kite-boarding later today. I live in a small town a block off the beach because I want to be near the water, and I want to be near the water because I like surfing-related sports. And so my whole life has been geared toward things I love doing, and how I make a living is designed for what I like doing so I don't have to work all the time so I can be free to do what I want."

25

Misfits of the World, Unite!

There are so many outcasts out there and more ways to connect than ever before that this point in time feels sort of magical. In a few seconds and a few swipes we can discover new subcultures, hear authentic voices tell their stories, link up and feel welcomed by members of other outsider groups. True, the number of insecure bullies out there honing their demonizing skills are legion, passing laws to restrict expression, fighting to keep tradition unchanged as if the world around us isn't in a state of constant flux. It seems that some status quo storm troopers are hard at work manufacturing reasons why we are different, while misfits find themselves increasingly stumbling over similarities.

There are still "No Skateboarding" signs posted everywhere, but that doesn't stop skaters from finding new friends almost every time they hit a skate spot. I never know who will be at a skatepark anymore—a girl on roller skates, a guy in his forties skating for the first time in years, a world-famous pro, a ragamuffin kid riding a destroyed board, a gaggle of elementary school girls with pink helmets and tutus. While reviewing the final edits of this book, I snuck in a session and a smiling wrinkled gentleman rolled up to the bowl. Fully padded up and skating at a slower pace, we began talking and it came out that he was over sixty years old. This wasn't a former world-class pro, wired with exceptional physical gifts—this was a typical person that was exceptional in how they never stopped connecting to their passion.

It's never too late to find your inner misfit and plug yourself back into the freak terminal to feel that non-regulated juice zapping through you again. Michelle sees this all the time when people lace up again after losing touch with roller-skating. "We have customers that have taken a long break come in and put on their skates and . . ." Michelle takes a long, slow inhale and her shoulders drop dramatically at the reconnection. "They roll around and say, 'I forgot about this! This is soooooooo good!'"

In Brooklyn, it's the same for the people shuffling Magic: the Gathering cards or rolling dice to discover a spell's damage. "I can't tell you how many people my age have come into the store and said, 'I wish I had a place like this when I was a kid,'" Dr. Jon says. "And I say, 'I wish I did too!'" and then he invites them to find a "place like this" as an adult and join in the fun.

"I was trying to model Brooklyn Strategist after a brick-and-mortar store that had been in my neighborhood for twenty-five years and had recently closed its door," Dr. Jon says. "At its core, this store was a neighborhood communal space—they served food, had homemade ice cream, desserts. You could walk into that space and see grandparents hanging with grandkids, adults reading papers, you could see the heavily tattooed and a body-pierced person behind the counter—it brought all cross-cultural generations together in the space. After it closed, I thought what the neighborhood really needed was something like that. One of the MOs of my business was how do I create a community space that is safe for everyone. It wasn't very long after I opened my doors that non-cis people started finding their way in and recognizing that they weren't being judged, that it was safe to be who they were, and that spread virally by word of mouth."

Roger would often go undercover at his Beyond the Streets shows to see how people were reacting to his cross-cultural communication. "I worked in the gift shop for a few hours every day," he says, "just getting people T-shirts and things like that. Very few people recognized me and I loved talking to people about the experience and what they saw. Talking to the multigenerational groups at shows where you have a husband and a wife and their parents and then a twelve-year-old kid were some of my favorite moments."

New generations have a beautiful way of mowing down the fence lines that obstruct the previous generation's worldview. "When you remove social taboos," Dr. Jon says, "how many more people are willing to acknowledge that's how they feel?" He points to the light-speed jump into technological lives that has warped social hierarchy. "I think nerdiness in general is more accepted, even, dare I say, a sexy quality, than when I was in high school and you'd get locked in the locker for that."

Digital platforms have the potential to megaphone individual voices, allowing them to penetrate traditional social soundproofing. In doing so, they reshape narratives that were long under the control of status quo guardians. So many outsiders are excelling at sharing the positives of their offset passions that it's inspiring others to participate.

"You encourage people to foster their scenes," Tony says. "Yes, we have a big skate world and yes, it's becoming more inclusive, but in those inclusive sets there are people fostering their own little scenes. There are local women's events and people organizing meetups every Thursday at a specific skatepark, which fosters a scene and encourages people that might be afraid to try it. I'll see a bunch of girls—some are just beginners, but they're all supporting each other. Grassroot efforts is how you truly grow your subculture, and social media is the great equalizer in how you find your crew, your scene, and like-minded individuals. That's been one of the best aspects of social media. There are plenty of terrible aspects, but the way it's connected outsiders throughout the world is one of the silver linings of all of it."

It is now common for multiple generations of misfits to participate in their fringe passions together. Besides getting energized by the creativity and energy of younger folk, the older generation sends a powerful message—this thing you love doing can continue all through life. Tony is a prime example, because of the physical nature of aging multiplied by the bodily damage caused by crashing on a skateboard.

Now, if it was all pure ego, then the focus on aging might zero in on what was lost. But what I've noticed with an older misfit like Tony is that he's once again cutting a path for others—how to live your passion at various stages of life. Once he turned fifty, the dude automatically re-

ceived AARP (American Association of Retired Persons) mail, but he's shown us all that he's still young enough to willingly take a slam in order to keep progressing.

The idea of a pro leading progressive skateboarding in their *late twenties* was absurd when Tony started rolling. "I just thought there was a certain age that you had to be 'responsible' and you wouldn't skate anymore," Tony says of how his young misfit brain thought in the early 1980s. "I figured it was around thirty. I saw a picture of a guy from Florida in a skate magazine and the caption read: 'So-and-so is thirty and still going!' I thought, *Whoa, he's thirty and doing inverts!* He set the limit by default. But when I was thirty, I thought, *What? Are you kidding? I'm learning more tricks than ever.*"

Tony spun the 900 when he was thirty-one and did his last one when he was forty-eight.

This misfit generational cross-boundary inspiration is everywhere now. DEVO played a sold-out fiftieth anniversary world tour. Gray-haired seniors in brightly colored eyeglasses and Energy Dome headwear were pogoing next to high schoolers, feeding off each other's stoke, singing in unison: "If you live in a small town, you might meet a dozen or two, young alien types who step out and dare to declare: We're through being cool!"

Young and old misfits were locking into the same vibe at vastly different times in their lives. Parents brought their kids and some kids brought their parents to see seventy-year-old men stomp around stage and sing about the universal state of de-evolution. DEVO may have started their weirdo rallying call back in the 1970s, way before many in the crowd were even born, but when a teenager looks to their side and sees a grandma with white hair styled into a New Wave coif wearing boxy nerd glasses dancing in rhythm with two thousand other oddballs of all types they know that misfits never need retire.

26

Misfit Parenting

As a teenager on a road trip with my dad, it was my turn to DJ, and I put on a mixtape with Stiff Little Fingers: "And they say they're a part of you, and that's not true, you know. They say they've got control of you, and that's a lie, you know. They say you'll never be free."

I'm not sure my dad could understand the punk song about teenage life in Belfast, written about "the sheer tedium of having nowhere to go and nothing to do when you got there," but he asked what kind of song this was. When I told him it was called "Alternative Ulster," Dad nodded and offered a critique: "Sounds like a guy fucking a tin can."

I loved my dad (and love my mom!). He didn't understand the nuances of skateboarding, but he never tried to make me quit, and I think he respected how it made you push yourself and care less about other people's judgments. Both my parents fully supported what was clearly making me happy, so much so that when an angry elderly neighbor demanded that they make me stop skateboarding near my house, my mom told him that was not going to happen.

Generations change, and parenting styles with them, but as a misfit father myself, it became readily apparent that the bulk of my duties was going to be making sure that my kids realized there were unfathomable ways to live life out there, regardless of how society tries to gaslight you into the standardized version. As my kids started going to school, swiping their phones, just generally algorithmed and marketed to death, my job became infinitely more difficult than I had imagined.

Conformity makes it easy to parent—follow instructions and do the same as the ones around you. Pay to join this travel league with other parents, not because your kid enjoys it or shows interest, but because it's now the new normal. Focus on earning a communal symbol of success to plaster over any individual traits. Pay for coaches, tutors, teachers—allow "experts" to be hired to instruct your child on the ways of the world. Corral them into activities solely to score scholarships or gain entrance into a certain university. Parental FOMO has evolved from missing authentic experiences into something akin to child abuse if you don't "support" your kid with all the marketed might available. Excelling at childhood has now become predatorily commercialized.

Go to school and then college, where it's permissible to go wild like previous generations did. In fact, you may be encouraged to replicate the same generational "wildness," by following the same rules for breaking rules, without realizing that it might be yet another standardized template that you're pouring yourself into.

Society's assembly line becomes even more frightening when you are constantly trying to keep a loved one off it. Again, there is nothing inherently conformist or nonconformist about doing an activity—it's *how* you do it that matters. Nowadays there are "skateboard coaches," after all. I have a relative who randomly took an Arabic language class at college, which changed her life, allowing her to find her passion of working with NGOs in the Middle East.

But finding an individual passion is a bit like . . . getting hit by a truck? For most of us it has the flavor of accidental chance, a blunt-force impact from out of nowhere, sending sense-of-self spiraling through the air. My older son, Cooper, skates and surfs. My youngest, Ronin, has zero interest in skating, and I realized there is no difference between a dad forcing his kid into baseball and a dad forcing his kid onto a skateboard. What I value about skateboarding, after all, disappears once you reduce it to its mere physicality.

This is where misfit wisdom comes into play as a parent. It helps to have an understanding of the haphazardness behind finding a passion and how parental control kills it dead. You can't orchestrate situations, because by doing that you are already directing the results. You can't simply transfer your experiences down a generation—it's already changed too much and there are cosmic safeguards against such cheap duplication.

Stacy went from being one of the first professional skateboarders to a brand owner to a documentary director, always seeking out new ways to express himself. He did it physically through skating and surfing, took up drawing and painting later in life, got his fingers dirty and created a garden that garnered newspaper articles. In other words, he's pretty well rounded, with a wide variety of interests for his kid to latch on to.

"Take your cues from your kid," Stacy says when asked what he did when his son, Austin, expressed interest in a world Stacy knew nothing about—the piano. "My position was not to tell my kid what to do, but to give him all the options so that he could do what he did—that was the point. Also, paying attention to what he was doing was vital. For instance, my son started with classical music and immediately became good at it, but I could tell he wanted to go off-page and improvise."

Stacy, while not as musically inclined as his son, was still aware of the process of discovery, and reached out for help. "I went to two friends of mine with musical backgrounds and explained my predicament, and they told me to get him an Oscar Peterson CD and a Red Garland CD. I brought them home and Austin played them and became really intrigued. That was when he was nine years old. By age fourteen he was playing the Tokyo Jazz Festival. I was simply paying attention to what he was doing. I didn't tell him to do it, I just said, 'I think you might like this.'"

I think you might like this . . . and then recede into the background and let the discovery happen out of your control. Beautiful. As a parent, I know how much discipline it takes to do that. And I know I've bungled many of my kids' discoveries by not getting out of the way fast enough. "Find out what your kid is interested in," Stacy says. "That's the key. If the kid doesn't know, then help them go out and experience a variety of things until they find out what interests them."

27

The Kids Are More Than All Right

I rolled up to the skatepark a few years ago and it was as if I'd wormholed into an alternate universe. Around the bowl usually populated with veteran skaters were around ten pink, yellow, and bright baby blue helmets bobbing around at half the height of the normal crowd, some with pink mohawk dinosaur spikes, almost all with crazy stickers or rainbow patterns. The excited, high-pitched giggling of young girls projected a very different soundtrack into the area.

Most of the girls looked about fourth-grader age and apparently had arranged weekly meetups at the skatepark. Clustered together, they encouraged one other, jumping and clapping and cheering wildly when one of them broke a personal barrier. In no way were they looking at the older, more experienced male skaters for social cues or any sort of guidance on how to act.

Skateparks can be intimidating for the newcomer, old and young alike. Maybe it feels like all the locals are tight and you're interloping, maybe there are insecurities about being judged (not just newbies—I know top pros who feel uncomfortably judged at skateparks), but this group of girls had transformed the area into another atmosphere completely by their approach.

They simply charged, approaching the skatepark like a playground, with no concerns if they were doing it "right" or if they looked cool—they were out to have fun. It was one of the raddest tricks I have ever seen. In a totally new state of exploration, they were discovering new sensations at a blistering pace.

One of them saw something that an older skater did out of the pool and started trying something like it at a very low level below the coping, grabbing her board differently. Then others in the gang jumped in and started trying it as a group in a variety of ways. One of them almost did something not at all like the original trick and walked out of the bowl saying, with no ego or boasting, "I'm getting better!" Were they talking to themselves or the gang? Did it matter?

These girls were making their own scene. They had entered a very tight, pressurized culture with a storied history and couldn't have cared less. It was so awesome. They clearly didn't read *Thrasher* magazine and weren't up-to-date on all the new videos, hot new pros, trendy tricks, probably didn't know any pro skater names, and it was obvious that they didn't see the reason why any of that was necessary.

All they needed was each other and a skateboard. It was one of the purest connections to skating I had seen in a long while. A group of inexperienced, hyper, elementary school–age girls showed me something I was missing with skating.

"I stand to benefit from creative people who are different," Sacha says. "I still recognize that in people. It's cool. That's what keeps you on your toes and keeps you fresh—connecting with younger folks who are kinda going through what you went through thirty years ago."

Nostalgia is a hell of a drug. Like many drugs, it can give users a closed-off, surreal experience while making them super annoying to anybody forced to deal with their shit. Is there anything that disconnects a cultural connection faster than a more historied person telling you how much better it was, you know, before you even had a chance to be here? What is any newcomer supposed to do with that information?

When older misfits think that way, express that sentiment, we're locking ourselves in a prison of preciousness. As pointed out earlier, misfit cultures are in a constant state of evolution, always reacting against oppressive pressure, even when that comes from within. It's a defense mechanism designed to protect against unintentionally hardening into a traditional, conventional activity.

For the next few weeks I checked myself for calcified approaches and views, and found plenty. It takes a lot of effort to continually open yourself up to discovery when you are obsessed with a culture over a lifetime. I found many shortcuts and assumptions that had slowly become fossil-

ized. A gang of little girls had taken on the guru role and showed me what I had been missing.

In a fresh twist, many misfit cultures are being used to sprout intricate new subcultures—micro subgroups misfitting within a broader misfit culture. There are gay and trans skateboard teams. The Brooklyn Strategist hosts queer night and makes it clear that how one misfits from the general population isn't the important part. Skateboard legends like Brian Anderson and Elissa Steamer ripped as two of the most popular professionals, but it seemed that the changes ushered in by a new generation allowed them to come out and be celebrated as queer and enjoy the full support of major mainstream and core sponsors.

Roller-skating is a prime example of an entire subculture being organically recoded by a new generation to reflect current views. "The 1990s hate and homophobia toward Rollerbladers was not the first time that shoe skaters were considered gay," Michelle says. "There are lots of gays in roller-skating. Roller-skating is very queer, very *proud*. I think gays have a way of killing the resistance to be themselves by expressing themselves, and because roller-skating encourages that it's an easy way to be yourself and express yourself."

And new solutions are being created to meet new challenges. "I organize the biggest roller-skating competition," Michelle says. "Roller-skating has a large population of transgender or queer athletes. Eight percent of our customer base identify as nonbinary or trans. That is really difficult to navigate when you're signing people up for divisions in a contest, so we don't have men's or women's contests—everybody competes together. We have people sign up for which prize they want to accept at the end of the contest. So everyone competes together, but when it comes time to divide prizes, we take the top women's score, the top men's score,

the top nonbinary score, and at the end of the contest we have three podiums."

"They're expanding the reach and inclusivity," Tony says of the newer generations, visibly excited about learning what he can from them. "They are taking the foundation and doing things we never imagined with it. It's like a collective evolution."

28

Gratitude

It was one of those significant birthdays that bring people together, and around two dozen of us, from teenagers to technically "senior citizens," were sitting around a long table in a room at a Japanese restaurant. A very strong gathering of styles, careers, and lifestyles. All were regaled with absurd stories about playing European goth shows in subterranean caves, accidentally farting in front of rock stars, a stadium crowd chanting "Son of a bitch!" in unison at a famous misfit too sick to perform.

One guest who has dyed his hair in an unbroken chain of Manic Panic colors since last century remembered a time as a teenager when a fellow skateboarder met him outside a skatepark, eager to share the excitement of another friend's new trick. Unwilling to stand for any dilly-dallying, the friend simply picked him up and carried him to the bowl to share in the witnessing and subsequent celebration of a barrier being broken.

Someone remembered how the friend that had furniture-moved his buddy would post anonymous classified ads in the local newspaper purely for his own enjoyment: "CEILING FAN—yellow and gray, blades come off on high speed, otherwise good."

The room filled with the laughter and warmth of relationships in a constant state of connective reweaving through dark humor, parallel experiences, and a type of shared joy that fizzes up from the surprise of thriving within an unexpected life.

Mid-laugh, a shiver ran through me, the kind that feels as if your body had iced a cycle of blood, physiological reaction arriving before conscious reasoning. Thoughts did follow a moment later, playing like a scrambled horror movie trailer: *What if I had come into this world and felt . . . normal? What if all my muscles, fat, cartilage clumped together in all the right places, drawing admiring second glances from strangers? What if I didn't constantly mispronounce new words? What if I watched* Repo Man *and the lines "Let's go do those crimes" and "Yeah. Yeah! Let's go get sushi and not pay" did not evoke deep spiritual laughter? What if I had never been jettisoned into a voyage of discovery with all these rad people around me?*

My life suddenly appeared as one unstable, towering Jenga game, pieces pulled and stacked in precarious, seemingly haphazard ways. One ill-placed or ill-pulled block—dating a popular high schooler, displaying a talent for catching footballs, relating to the pretty lovers in *St. Elmo's Fire* instead of the "slacker" McFly in *Back to the Future*—and my life might have toppled into a collective conventional pile instead of feeling as if it was often teetering in a glorious anticipatory, swaying tilt.

Another cycle of iced blood: *I wouldn't even have realized it.*

Wait a sec . . . Is this the same sentiment all the popular kids at school think when they see us misfits doing our own weird thing as we wandered the frays of the social wastelands?

It was a stupid feeling. I'm legit ashamed to have felt it. It's not as if being a misfit is empirically better in any way than an embrace of conventionality. It's more that there was never any choice in being a misfit, which made me feel even *more* grateful. This was never asked for. I didn't follow any master design. Like all of us misfits, we were just trying to persist.

I sat there playing with my chopsticks, wondering what was going on inside my head while everyone was still laughing about "blades come off on high speed, otherwise good" when it hit: Maybe the crossed wires in my brain take the neurological pathways less traveled to get to what I finally realized was the destination: Gratitude. Gratitude with a capital G.

My brain pulled up a piece of conversation with Ed to provide commentary: "That's the deformer. That's why I used that as a title for one of my books. That's the word for how you get shaped."

Is this how devastating gratitude presents itself to everyone? I've felt grateful so many times before, but this divided perspective into momentary duality, one part participating in the action while another part observed and appreciated the specialness of it in the same moment.

It was a disorienting sensation, giddy in unexpectedness but also communal, because I knew that every single person in that room was equally surprised by their lives. How do negatives and positives work when they add up to an answer that deftly avoids either binary categorization? **I'd always been taught gratitude was thankfulness, but this was different—this was an awe of how life works.**

What was responsible for the part of us that fought from who knows when to navigate according to some unseen map? That part of us that never gave up, even when we wanted to. I remember laughing with Stacy when he said he was furious with himself that bowling hadn't been enough, that that unknown part of himself had dragged him through anxiety, stress, exhaustion to get him to his singular misfit joy.

What had Tony said when I asked him about the misfit label? "It's the label I would embrace the most," he said. "I don't want to hide from it, and I'd encourage others to embrace it in their own way because when you break free of expectations and tradition, then you can do anything."

Expectations. The misfit life taught all of us to be wary of them. I had thought that was because we had repeatedly been told to lower ours, but what the misfit cycle actually does when followed through to the end is transcend expectations.

I looked around at a table of outcasts bonded in a way that I never imagined possible, and something Sacha said over and over in our conversations echoed through me: **"I can promise you, none of this shit was planned. None of it. There was no way I could plan it."**

ACKNOWLEDGMENTS

Writing a book can be a strange experience. You start alone and then you send it to somebody and they decide if they want anything to do with it and then they ask other somebodies if they want to join in. It feels as if you're asking people to all squeeze into a small life raft and cast off for a year or so without much navigational equipment. Maybe it's fun, and you find some pirate treasure and bring it all back home. Or maybe you get lost, and you bitch at each other and your skin starts to peel from the sun and to stave off starvation you end up eating each other. I've had both experiences. On this book, the life raft was full of pretty awesome people who helped steer it into exciting new territories that I wouldn't have found on my own, and I am grateful for sharing the experience with them. Mary Reynics is a kickass editor, with strong navigational skills and the confidence to encourage others to have a say. I hope Penguin/Random House/Ballantine is paying her a million dollars a year. Roger Freet was my agent. He quoted *Repo Man* and had a degree in divinity. A special blend. He hyped this book and then he died. I miss talking to him. RIP, buddy. Phil Marino keeps talking to me about football like I know what a first down is, but he is down for the oddballs and backed this project from the start. Ivanka Perez has editorial gut feelings that make me jealous. If I ever figure out a novel I'm going to be knocking on her door. Tony, I'm sorry you look like a victim of bad lip filler in my drawing of you at the front of the book. Diane Hobbing embraced the misfit message and created a design radiating a passionate DIY vibe that added another layer to the book. Of course, thanks to Tony, Stacy, Sacha, Roger, Dr. Jon, Michelle, Stecyk, Seneca, Mark, Brian, Mat, Ed, and Shepard for sharing their singular perspectives. Hi Mom. And C. R. Stecyk III! Besides being a heavy life influence, he allowed me to riff on his iconic BONES hazard sign for the cover of this book. In typical C.R. fashion, he replied to my request with some seemingly unrelated photos (although, with his brain, who can tell) and a "Feel free to do so." Finally, Francesca, Cooper, and Ronin, for tolerating me cluttering up the family kitchen table with notebooks and scraps of brainstormed thoughts and piles of pencil shavings even though I have a perfectly fine desk and office that I never use.

ACKNOWLEDGMENTS

ABOUT THE AUTHOR

Sean Mortimer was a sponsored skateboarder. He wrote some books including *HAWK: Occupation: Skateboarder* (coauthored with Tony Hawk), and *The Mutt: How to Skateboard and Not Kill Yourself* (coauthored with Rodney Mullen). He lives in Southern California with his wife and sons.

IG: @judoair

ABOUT THE TYPE

This book was set in Garamond, a typeface originally designed by the Parisian type cutter Claude Garamond (c. 1500–61). This version of Garamond was modeled on a 1592 specimen sheet from the Egenolff-Berner foundry, which was produced from types assumed to have been brought to Frankfurt by the punch cutter Jacques Sabon (c. 1520–80).

Claude Garamond's distinguished romans and italics first appeared in *Opera Ciceronis* in 1543–44. The Garamond types are clear, open, and elegant.

Whoa, don't let these boring blank pages go to waste. Work on your graffiti name. Draw some haircut ideas. Write a song. Design a protest poster. Create your own skateboard graphics even if you don't skateboard. Draw a cartoon strip. Start writing your own book.